TRUST YOURSELF FIRST

TRUST YOURSELF FIRST

Cultivating Self-Awareness, Confidence and Resilience

Doris Sew Hoy

NEW DEGREE PRESS

TRUST YOURSELF FIRST
Cultivating Self-Awareness, Confidence and Resilience

ISBN
979-8-88504-078-5   *Paperback*
979-8-88504-707-4   *Kindle Ebook*
979-8-88504-186-7   *Digital Ebook*

To my family:

Simon, Sara-Louise (Sasa),
Lucinda (Lulu), and Mylo.

My parents, Yip and Lai Kum Sew Hoy,
and my grandparents, YeYe and MaMa.

And Esther, Wallace, Jack, Helen,
Fiona, Shona, and Kevin.

THE

WAY

OUT

IS

IN

THÍCH NHẤT HẠNH
October 11, 1926-January 22, 2022

CONTENTS

ADVANCED REVIEWS FOR TRUST YOURSELF FIRST

"Excellent—clear, concise, comprehensive, and timely as many of us wrestle with who we are and what we really want to do. This book is an investment in ourselves."

–MIKE BRENT, PROFESSOR OF PRACTICE AT HULT INTERNATIONAL BUSINESS SCHOOL AND CO-AUTHOR OF *THE LEADER'S GUIDE TO INFLUENCE.*

"Seamlessly weaves together ideas, stories, and learnings with an engaging style that feels like a personal conversation, inviting you to learn more about yourself."

–GINA CAMPBELL, AUTHOR OF *HOPE IN A CORNER OF MY HEART: A HEALING JOURNEY THROUGH THE DREAM-LOGICAL WORLD OF INNER METAPHORS.*

"A refreshing book filled with resourceful activities we can implement for ourselves and share with others. Having worked with Doris, I can attest that she walks her talk on cultivating healthy—and vital—relationships."

–SHARON SMALL, FOUNDER OF CLEAN LANGUAGE INSTITUTE, USA.

"An authentic writer who opens her heart to you. I particularly like the key messages and reflective questions at the end of each chapter; helps you explore and connect with yourself more deeply and to trust yourself more fully."

–JULIA FENG, POSITIVE CHANGE COACH OF POSITIVE CHANGE PRACTITIONERS CENTER, PHILIPPINES.

"A must-read for anyone yearning to discover more about what makes them tick. Delivers a tour-de-force lesson in how to better trust ourselves, harness our potential, and unleash our inner leaders."

–DAN MAGILL, UX WRITER AND COMMUNICATIONS CONSULTANT.

"So authentic and powerful, especially loved the chapter on Compassion is Caring which was handled so clearly and sensitively and really resonated. The book gives me the vocabulary to articulate feelings, understand why they are there, and how to deal with them."

–TIGGY MUNNELLY, VOLUNTEER TEACHER AT MYANMAR EDUCATION CENTRE, KUALA LUMPUR.

- Communication – the glue connecting the three other Cs; includes listening receptively and maintaining confidentiality.

4C MODEL OF TRUST

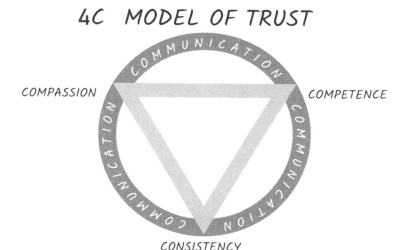

COMPASSION   COMPETENCE

CONSISTENCY

When we can be more compassionate about the many parts of ourselves, commit to improve our competence, and commit to showing up consistently with the best of intentions, then we will learn to trust ourselves more and build healthy and trusting relationships with others.

Think about applying these four components to yourself in different aspects of your life. For example, when I think of my relationship with myself when I'm playing golf, I realize I am very consistent when it comes to showing up to play with someone. Once a date and time are agreed upon, I'll be there; however, in terms of consistency in my ability and skill when playing the game, that can vary considerably.

I need to work on being more compassionate and caring to myself, especially when it comes to how I talk to myself. "Stupid idiot!" is what you might hear me utter as the ball goes flying off to one side. This probably equates to my level of competence in golf—not very high!

How we talk to ourselves is indicative of the relationship we have with ourselves. There's value in making an assessment about our efforts, with a view to working out what we can do to improve. I need to be more realistic about where my competence or skill level is in golf and be a little less critical of my own performance. That applies not only in this game of golf, but in other areas of my life.

We all have an "inner critic," that voice at the back of our minds that pops up when times get tough. Some inner critics can be very harsh and see things only in absolute terms with no room for nuance or grey areas. "You should just give up," that critic may say. "You're no good" or "you're so useless."

Some of these thoughts are related to Imposter Syndrome: the self-limiting belief you are not as competent as others believe you are. This is not uncommon, especially amongst high achieving women. In fact, an estimated 70 percent of people experience these feelings at some point in their lives, according to a review article in the *International Journal of Behavioral Science*.

TRUST VERSUS TRUSTWORTHINESS

The word "trust" is used often, yet many people have misconceived views about trust. Philosopher Onora O'Neill makes an important distinction about context when it comes to trust and trustworthiness: it depends on the situation and the person. It's not simply a matter of trusting or not trusting, but how much to trust about what with whom. As she says in her 2013 TED talk, "I would aim to have more trust in

- When you trust yourself, you can allow yourself to be more vulnerable with others and initiate actions to trust others more.

- Building trust with another is a two-way process: the more you trust someone, the more they are likely to trust you.

- You can lead the way by keeping your word, delivering on your promises, and apologizing when you've made a mistake or misunderstood something.

- Your turn. Think about a relationship you care about and want to develop. Applying my 4C model of trust, ask yourself:

  - Consistency: how reliable and honest am I in this relationship?

  - Compassion: how much do I really care about this relationship? How is that care demonstrated?

  - Competency: what knowledge, skills, and experience do I have and bring to this relationship? Where do I want to improve?

  - Communication: how well do I listen? How comfortable am I to speak up, especially when things go wrong? How well can I maintain confidentiality?

My family, with MaMa and YeYe on the left and my parents on the right. Taken around 1968, all dressed up to attend a wedding function.

I'm number six out of eight siblings, with two older brothers, three older sisters, one younger sister, and a younger brother. I grew up in an intergenerational household. My paternal grandparents lived with us, and, like many Chinese families, played a pivotal parenting role as my parents worked in our market garden most of the time.

My grandma, MaMa, was an expert seamstress and knitter. She made all the clothes for the family, and I learned my sewing skills from her, though I never quite mastered knitting. My grandfather, YeYe, was an amazing baker; very methodical and precise. I later learned he used to work in a bakery in Hong Kong during the 1930s before immigrating to New Zealand. He was a quiet man who knew English and diligently read the *Otago Daily Times* newspaper each day. Whenever he came across a word he didn't know or thought was interesting, he'd circle it. I think it was his way of building his English vocabulary while also encouraging my siblings and me to build ours.

Home was one large, extended family setting in a solid two-story house built by a Scottish pioneer to Otago. I remember our mealtimes as fast and furious, with us younger ones piling our rice bowls with tasty bits of meat and florets of fresh vegetables from our garden as accompaniments. We'd then sit at a side table or eat in front of the TV in the living room, thus allowing the elders—my grandparents, parents, uncle and older siblings—to sit around the dinner table.

We all worked on the market garden from a very young age. After school, I'd change into my work clothes, have something to eat, then go out and do whatever needed doing: hoeing weeds and planting or harvesting cabbages, cauliflower, potatoes, etc. Admittedly, I resented having to work every day after school, as that wasn't what other kids in my class did, but then again, I didn't really know what other kids did after school. The boys tended to make the occasional derogatory racist remark, to which I'd pretend not to notice and tell myself they were just stupid and ignorant.

FEELING LIKE AN OUTSIDER

I've always felt like an outsider. This is especially the case when I started school where being Chinese was clearly a minority. At home, my brothers, sisters, and I spoke only Cantonese with our parents and grandparents, but we could not read or write Chinese. When I started school, I learned English as a second language. As many immigrant children know from experience, learning another language when you're young and immersed in it isn't particularly difficult.

Even within my own family, I often felt like I didn't fit in. I think this was because I was the sixth youngest sibling and didn't have nearly as much to say. My older siblings could all talk and express their views in no uncertain terms—fast and furious, a bit like our mealtimes!

Being one of the youngest in a family of strong and confident personalities, I like to think I developed my capacity to listen and observe people from an early age. Although, having said that, my siblings would be quick to remind me about my knack for falling asleep at any time of the day!

Whatever I may think about my siblings, we are family and have become closer as the years pass by, and particularly more so since the COVID-19 pandemic. We're located all around the world: me in the UK, youngest sibling Kevin in Hong Kong, oldest brother Wallace in Australia, and the rest spread throughout New Zealand in Auckland, Palmerston North, and Wellington. Like many families scattered over the world, we now keep in touch almost daily via a WhatsApp group chat and the occasional video call. On such calls, I often find myself acting as the facilitator in order to ensure there is one voice speaking at any one time; otherwise it can be a bit like a work meeting, or even a parish council, where everyone thinks they have the authority to speak first!

LEAVING HOME

My feeling like an outsider, both at school and within my own family, led me on my quest to discover my own identity. I'd often ask myself, "Who am I?" I really didn't know. Or, more precisely, the things I knew about myself somehow didn't resonate. They were just too superficial: my name, my home country, my place in my family, where I went to school. While all factually true, I felt so much nuance was missing. I hoped that one day, somehow, I'd find the key to unlocking who I really was, and maybe even my destiny or purpose in life. It wasn't long before I spotted an opportunity to begin my quest.

When I was twelve, I saw a poster at my local high school advertising a cultural exchange program called American Field Service (AFS). One of my brother's friends had just returned from spending a year in an American high school as an AFS scholar. I thought, *if he can do that, so can I.*

So, at sixteen, I applied and was accepted. It was the first time I left home. I traveled to St. Louis, Missouri, settled in with my new American family, and attended Clayton High School as a senior. Everything was new to me: navigating a big city, the huge extremes in temperature each season, the food, and the people. No one expected me to speak English as fluently as I did, and I'd have fun leading people on: "Yes, we Chinese. Fast learner."

One of the things I liked most about this experience was the fact that no one knew anything about me apart from my name and where I came from. I was free to be however I wanted to be. I enjoyed being just another student, although, of course, I wasn't. But this time, there was a distinct advantage in being different. As an international student on a cultural exchange program, I represented New Zealand, my home country. The fact I was Chinese helped dispel any preconceived ideas my host country had about New Zealanders, and probably also about Chinese people! I made friends there and am still in touch with many. My American friends had very different outlooks, experiences, and expectations compared to my few friends in New Zealand, and I found the differences refreshing.

After my year abroad, I returned to New Zealand, studied economics at Otago University, then moved to Wellington for my first permanent job. I worked as part of a small team of scientists and economists forecasting and planning energy demand and supply. Two years later, I left New Zealand again, this time heading to the UK on a Commonwealth Scholarship for post-graduate studies at Durham University in the north of England.

I eventually ended up in London's financial heart, the City or Square Mile, joining the London Stock Exchange as an economist in 1986. This was just before "Big Bang" when the Exchange moved from a floor-based securities trading market to an electronic screen-based one. A decade passed as my career as an economist analyzing the impact of deregulation in the securities market progressed, and eventually transitioned into developing markets in Russia and Vietnam and latterly as the Exchange's first Head of Internal Communications.

TWIST AND TURNING POINT

How I came to this latter role was an unexpected twist and one which, in hindsight, marked a turning point in my career. I believed the role was one needed in the organization, as the industry and the business had undergone significant and drastic change, structurally and operationally, in a few years. I was well-aware that most employees had a poor understanding of how their roles related and connected to the overall business and success of the organization.

I remember vividly how I went to see the director of Human Resources, a rather stern woman with a reputation for being somewhat standoffish. Despite that, I wanted to make sure one of the requirements for the role was a thorough understanding of how securities markets and the Exchange's businesses actually work, as I was getting annoyed at the number of times I had to correct people's misinformation and misunderstandings about how the markets worked. To my surprise, she turned to look at me and asked, "Would you be interested in applying for this role, Doris?"

Would I? I'd not considered myself as a candidate and my initial reaction was, "No, not really." My expertise and experience was about markets and analyzing the efficiency and effectiveness of systems and operations. This role was about educating, informing, and motivating people in the workplace, without any direct line management authority.

But as I thought about it more, I realized this was an opportunity to put into practice what I had long believed and observed: when people understand more about how what they do matters in the overall chain of delivery, they are more self-motivated. A key deliverable of the role would be to ensure regular internal communications about the business and its people—who was doing what, where, and why it mattered.

While I'd never envisaged myself in such a role before, I realized I ticked the box in terms of understanding the business, probably more so than most other candidates. I could see how the role would help in the development of others, as well as developing myself. This was the incentive that got me to apply. I thought, if the recruitment panel trusted me enough to appoint me, then I knew I could (or at least, I would have to) trust myself to deliver.

During my three years as Head of Internal Communications, I augmented my practical experiences in employee engagement and organizational development by studying for a master's in organizational behavior at Birkbeck College, University of London. That was also part of my plan to eventually move out of the corporate setting and into a more pragmatic academic role. I'd find this role at Ashridge, now part of Hult International Business School, an executive educational trust, where I joined the faculty to teach and lead business development and marketing programs.

WHO ARE YOU NOW?

I was young when I first started pondering the "Who am I?" question. Now that I'm older and hopefully a little wiser, I believe a better question is, "What's your sense of who you are now?" This question accurately captures us as we are now. Yes, of course we have a past and a future, but now, this present point in time, is really all there is, ever. As spiritual teacher Eckhart Tolle says, "Remember that the present is all you have. Make 'now' the center of your life."

What is my sense of who I am now? In 2022, my sense is I am my own best friend and someone who supports and develops others to become a better friend to themselves and others. I've learned to trust myself more and first. That trust was gradually built over several years based on experience and is born out of the belief that what I have to say matters; to myself and to others. Writing this book has helped me to understand my own journey and it is a way of sharing the learning to help you to trust yourself more.

Begin by asking yourself, "Where do you come from?" and map out your chronological past and where you have been geographically. Examine and investigate what happened, where, and with whom. Pinpoint the twists and turns in your life that have helped shape who you are today. Recognize the role that "bad" things and feelings have had. By reviewing your past about your family, your home country and where else you have been, your first job, etc., I hope you come to realize that these are not just stepping stones to something greater, but testaments to your adaptability and self-awareness. This is part of "knowing thyself" more.

KEY MESSAGES

- Locating the places where you were born and where else you have been since birth is a way of remembering your past and how you came to be where you are now.

- Associated with physical locations are people, events, and memories.

- Remembering and appreciating "where" you came from and where you have been contributes to you knowing yourself more, and that aspect of self-awareness adds to your capacity to cultivating more trust in yourself.

- Your turn:

  - Where do you come from?

  - How did you get from there to where you are now?

  - What roles have you played in your life and career?

  - What turning points have there been in your life?

Eastwood is part Māori, and has found his heritage to be a key factor in his life and work with teams such the Command Group of NATO, the South African cricket team, elite ballet, and more. He realized he could apply some of the spiritual ideas he'd grown up with and their ancient wisdom to these high-performing environments. One key spiritual idea is of "belonging and *whakapapa*"—you belong to something greater than yourself. When you're part of a team, it's the team's performance that matters most in achieving success.

Eastwood used the metaphor of the sun to bring this idea to life: a story of how the sun slowly moved down a chain of people from our first ancestor through the generations to our own family.

> "When the Sun shines on us, that's our time when we are alive... What is critical in our tribe is that they pass on to us our sense of identity, a sense of purpose, a vision of what we're trying to do together and our values and rituals and traditions." (Eastwood, 2020)

His words resonated with me, but it wasn't until I had a coaching session with my own coach and mentor, Angela Dunbar, that I realized how my heritage was having a much bigger impact on me. As we came near to the end of the session, Angela asked me, "What do you know now?"

I found myself declaring I knew my ancestors, who came to New Zealand in the late 1800s, were there to support me. I looked at Angela and told her I had no idea where my realization came from despite having spoken the words. What I did know was I had a new sense of curiosity beginning to stir inside me and a desire to learn more about my heritage.

MY CHINESE HERITAGE

It didn't take me long to trace my genealogy to the Ming Dynasty, thanks to all the work undertaken by my great uncle Justin Sew Hoy and other family members. They compiled an impressive Sew Hoy family tree book and subsequently digitized in a website to allow for ongoing updates.

Looking at my family tree, I finally see where I fit in in relation to my other cousins and relatives. Whilst both my parents are Chinese, I have many relatives who are mixed race, being part-Chinese, part Māori and/or part Caucasian. It was my grandfather's grandfather, Choie Sew Hoy, who originally immigrated to New Zealand in 1868 to work in the goldfields of Central Otago. Before coming to New Zealand, he'd labored in the goldfields of California and in Victoria, Australia. As I learned more about his journeys around the world over 150 years ago, I could only imagine the kind of stamina and resolve he had to endure those months-long voyages to new lands so far from his home.

I wondered to what extent my desire to travel beyond the hills and over the seas was something I inherited from my great-great-grandfather, albeit for quite different motives. His travels were for economic reasons, to support his family back in China. My travels were for purely personal, and rather selfish, reasons: I was in search of the answer to the question, "Who am I?" But I hope he'd be at least a little proud of me anyway, for traveling the world in search of something greater than myself, just as he did for his family. I like to believe I have inherited his global perspective and his initiative.

Though I know quite a lot about my paternal lineage, I know less about my mother's side. My mother was number twelve out of eighteen siblings; her father had three wives, sequentially. Like herself after marriage, many of her siblings to explore and experiment, try new things, talk with people you don't normally speak to, and see what happens. I did this when I signed up for the AFS program in high school. Being curious and having an open mind helps, and we'll explore more about this in chapter ten.

APPLYING THE MODEL

Another question I hear often is, "How do I decide what 'Hidden' bits of myself to disclose to others, and thus widen the Arena?"

This is where trust comes in—do you trust yourself enough to disclose something more about yourself you've previously kept hidden? This decision comes down to your capacity and choice to become more vulnerable, which in turn is about courage and belief in yourself.

This reminds me of Theodore Roosevelt's words about daring greatly, which I first read about in Brené Brown's book, *Dare to Lead*:

> "It is not the critic who counts; not the man who points out how the strong man stumbles, or where the doer of deeds could have done them better. The credit belongs to the man who is actually in the arena, whose face is marred by dust and sweat and blood; who strives valiantly; who errs, who comes short again and again, because there is no effort without error and shortcoming; but who does actually strive to do the deeds; who knows great enthusiasms, the great devotions; who spends himself in a worthy cause; who at the best knows in the end the triumph of high achievement, and who at the worst, if he fails, at least fails while daring greatly, so that his place shall never be with those cold and timid souls who neither know victory nor defeat."

I immediately noticed Roosevelt's use of the word "arena." I don't know if Luft and Ingram were influenced by Roosevelt's quote in choosing "arena" as their label for that part of their Johari Window, but it seems very apt. It acknowledges the strength it takes to show more of yourself to the world, to this giant arena full of people, knowing some might criticize and denigrate you for what you dare to say or do, and yet you choose to do so because you trust yourself, your skills, your potential, and you trust in your *whakapapa* to have your back.

KEY MESSAGES

- Nature and nurture play a role in who you are. Knowing more about your genealogy (if possible) and your family history can provide insights in how you've developed and what, if any, personality traits you've inherited.

- While your past has shaped who you are, it doesn't define who you will become. You have choices.

- By becoming more self-aware, you develop self-confidence and appreciation of who you are and the type of person you would like to become.

- Your turn. Take time to reflect on these questions:

  - What do you know about your paternal and maternal lineage?

  - What traits or characteristics in your ancestors and heritage can you identify with in yourself?

- What do you know about yourself and how did you come to know these things?

- What do others say about you? How do these things compare with what you know about yourself?

- What would you like others to know about you that they may not?

An easy way to remember each: Think "S" in times of stress, then it's the sympathetic nervous system that kicks in. Think "P" in more peaceful times, then it's the parasympathetic nervous system in operation.

When danger is sensed, the ANS reacts immediately. It shifts from a calmer, thinking state to an alert state, ready to act. That readiness to act is often called the "fight or flight" response. Adrenaline pumps into our blood stream, our heart rate increases, and our breath becomes short and shallow. If these neuro-physiological responses reach an extreme overwhelm and overload stage, we can freeze, fragment from our memory, and collapse physically and mentally. This is the stage or state of trauma. (Low 2021)

THE POLYVAGAL THEORY AND PHYSIOLOGY

Let's take a closer look at the ANS by examining the polyvagal theory developed by Stephen Porges, professor of psychiatry at the University of North Carolina. At its core, the polyvagal theory is a more nuanced way of understanding the ANS. Porges' research explained how our bodies and brains interact with one another to regulate our physiological states, i.e., what is going on in our bodies, particularly in times of high stress.

He coined the term "neuroception" to refer to the constant and automatic process of the ANS, scanning for signs of safety or danger. His research showed neuroception happens before perception. In other words, our bodies (via the ANS) pick up danger signals in the environment first, way before our neo-cortex interprets bodily sensations into feelings like anxiety, panic, fear, and overwhelm. These interpretations are perceptions created by the neo-cortex, and how true or real such perceptions depends on one's ability to discern the context (Porges, 2017).

While in the modern world, there are no longer as many wild animals roaming outside as predators, there may still be predators in terms of people you don't or can't trust because you sense they are "out to get you" or threaten you, psychologically speaking. Regardless, your ANS will respond in the same way. It will mobilize, get you ready for fight or flight or even "fawn," i.e., expressing excessive compliments or praise to gain someone's approval or favor. In extreme overwhelm, it may "freeze": you faint, collapse, or submit.

Porges also identified another defense system: the vagus circuit, unrelated to the sympathetic nervous system but dependent on the parasympathetic nervous system. This circuit consists of the vagus nerve, which has many ("poly") branches and "wanders" to the internal organs below and above the diaphragm. The term *vagus* is Latin for "vagrant" or "wanderer."

Instead of the two-way binary state of either (1) the parasympathetic "rest and digest" or (2) the sympathetic "fight, flight, or fawn" state, Porges showed there is a hierarchical ladder of various autonomic states.

- When one is feeling safe, it is the *ventral vagal*, a part of the parasympathetic nervous system, that is activated.

- Moving down the ladder, when danger is sensed, it is the *sympathetic* nervous system activated or mobilized in readiness for "fight, flight or fawn."

- At the bottom of the ladder, when extreme stress or overwhelm occurs, it is the *dorsal vagal*, part of the vagus nerve and the parasympathetic nervous system, that is immobilized. This is the state of "freeze" when we play dead as a survival defense reaction.

Comparison of Polyvagal Theory and Model of Psyche

The Polyvagal Theory Developed by Professor Stephen Porges	Model of the Psyche Developed by Professor Franz Ruppert
Ventral Vagal State: - Feeling safe and calm - Able to access neo-cortex	**Healthy Self:** - Integrated mind and body - Sense of agency
Sympathetic State: - Mobilization - Sensing danger or fear - Fight, flight, or fawn	**Survival Self:** - Feeling stressed, anxious, worried - Adopts defensive shield or armor - Dissociation, denial, distraction, addiction, avoidance
Dorsal Vagal State: - Immobilization - Extreme danger or overwhelm - Freeze	**Trauma Self:** - Wound within our psyche - Extreme danger; painful memories - Collapse, fainting, burnout, submission

DEFINING TRAUMA

The words "trauma" and "traumatized" are used in everyday language to mean a variety of different things. "It was such a traumatic experience meeting the in-laws!" To avoid confusion, when I talk about trauma and being traumatized, I'm talking about a specific brain and neurological state, defined as "the lasting impact of the danger response on our neurophysiology" (Vaughan Smith 2019).

Trauma does not refer to a specific event or incident—it refers to the consequence of the experience. The word "trauma" comes from the Greek word for wound, and it is thus the "wounds" we are left with.

We can distinguish between two types: physical and psyche trauma (Vaughan Smith 2019).

- Physical trauma: might be the result of physical attack or an accident. In these types, we can see the wound: open wounds where the skin is torn, cut or punctured, or closed wounds where a blunt force causes severe bruising. For example, when I slipped on an icy step two years ago, I landed on my left shoulder and left side, broke my humerus bone, and had massive black and blue bruises on my left side.

- Psyche trauma: we cannot see the wound directly. What can be seen instead is behavior being replayed in the present moment relating to what happened in the past. This includes how we relate to others, how safe we feel, our thoughts, emotional responses, levels of stress, and our bodily experience. For example, if a teacher shouted at you when you were a child, that experience might have left a mark or scar on your psyche. Later in your adult life, when your boss or superior shouts at you, you might regress to behaving as if you were that child again, which might mean crying, cowering, or hyperventilating.

In terms of mental health and well-being, we are talking about the degree of psyche trauma experienced. Often, when we don't feel safe or feel we are being attacked (physically, psychologically, and/or verbally), it's our surviving self, armored in readiness to defend and protect the wounds of trauma from the past. Types of defensive strategies include:

- Dissociation: disconnecting from the "here and now" in response to an activation of past memories. The mind stops living in the present and goes somewhere else.

- Denial: refusing to accept something part of us knows to be true. The unconscious motivation is to deny our trauma.

- Other survival defenses: include illusions, addictions, distractions, control of self and others, rescuing, avoidance, mental illness, and somatization (i.e., the expression of emotional distress through physical symptoms).

TRAUMA EXISTS IN ALL OF US

Trauma is part of the human condition by virtue of being born—it exists in all of us. This was a fact I learned from integrative psychotherapist and author, Julia Vaughan Smith, in her book, *Coaching and Trauma*. For some, this trauma may be to a very small extent and relates to developmental trauma, or what happened to us up to the age of about five. For others, it could be consequences of what happened later in life, such as severe accidents, abuse, assaults, etc.

In an interview with Vaughan Smith, she explained developmental trauma in more detail: "...the issue is because our nervous system is so immature [when very young]. Then it's very sensitized to things in the environment, which it reads as being dangerous. And so, that leaves a marker, however faint or deep. That marker is like an old-fashioned LP record, the grooves in it. It's the response of the immature nervous system to triggers in the environment."

Childhood or developmental trauma is widely shared across class, race, and socioeconomic status. There are many reasons why developmental trauma can occur:

- Maternal or fetal distress during pregnancy

- The pregnancy may not have been wanted

- Mother and baby may have been separated (illness, hospitalization, premature birth, etc.)

- Parenting styles which control, smother, or ignore the child, or setting high demands on them

- Parents with physical and/or mental health problems

- Sexual abuse

- Going to boarding school at a very early age

- Being in hospital for long periods.

MORE ABOUT THE SURVIVAL SELF

I'm a coach, not a therapist. When clients come to me, it's normally their healthy self, dominating their psyche. But, as Vaughan Smith reminded me, we all have a part of us which carries trauma to some extent. We all have "buttons that can be pushed" that can trigger our survival self to rise.

I recognize now how my own survival self came to the forefront when I suffered from prolonged periods of very low mood and fatigue. At the time, I had two young children dependent on me to get them to school, take care of them and the house, etc. I found it so difficult to get out of bed and felt more than just tired. I dreaded going through the motions of being a mother and making small talk at the school gate with other mothers at drop-off and pick-up times. Somehow, I coped. There was no joy and no lightness; just a heavy foreboding and darkness within. I didn't have anything physically wrong with me, but how I wished I did. I believed at the time a physical ailment was acceptable, but not a mental illness. I was in denial.

I believe my denial stemmed from what used to be a widely held cultural conditioning prevalent pre-millennium, that being mentally ill was negative and to be mentally ill was "bad." If I was mentally ill, I was a bad person. That last statement reflects the kind of poor, illogical thinking reinforcing my denial and dissociation. I was imprisoned within my very own self-limiting and erroneous belief.

I now know my mixed-up belief was the basis for feeling shame: the shame of being mentally unwell and thus a bad person. Luckily, I have some close friends who noticed how I was struggling despite my attempts to put on a brave face and urged me to see a doctor. After being referred to a psychiatrist, I was diagnosed with clinical depression, prescribed medication, and began seeing a psychologist. With time, I got well and am now so very grateful for having gone through those very dark nights. My suffering was a turning point in my development, and led me to explore the more subjective, feeling side of my neurology which, until then, I had long neglected. More about that in part three.

BEING IN DRAMA

A useful way to characterize the types of behavior that might arise when we're feeling stressed out or when we're not getting what we want is the Karpman Drama Triangle, a social model of human interaction. Developed by Dr. Stephen B. Karpman in the late 1960s, the triangle consists of three roles and maps the destructive interaction occurring among people in conflict or drama-intense relationship transactions (Karpman 1968).

Karpman placed these three roles on an inverted triangle and referred to them as being the three aspects, or faces, of drama:

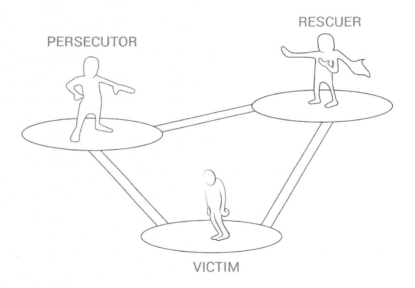

PERSECUTOR

RESCUER

VICTIM

- The Persecutor: The persecutor insists *it's all your fault.* The Persecutor is controlling, blaming, critical, oppressive, angry, authoritarian, rigid, and superior.

- The Victim: The victim in this model is not intended to represent an actual victim, but rather someone feeling or acting like one. The victim's stance is *poor me.* The victim feels oppressed, helpless, hopeless, powerless, ashamed, and seems unable to make decisions, solve problems, take pleasure in life, or achieve insight.

- The Rescuer: The rescuer's line is *let me help you.* Rescuers can feel guilty if they don't go to the rescue, yet their rescuing has negative effects: it keeps the victim dependent and doesn't allow the victim permission to fail or experience the consequences of their choices. The rewards for the rescuer are the focus is taken off them as they focus their energy on someone else, thus enabling them to ignore their own anxiety and issues. The rescuer's primary interest is really an avoidance of their own problems disguised as concern for the victim's needs.

When you are stressed and your nervous system is activated, you can find yourself bouncing around all three of those roles with someone, even in a single conversation or interaction. You are in a reactive mode and you are not accessing your higher order thinking processes. To step outside of the triangle, you firstly notice what's going on, especially with yourself.

Many people can self-identify as rescuers, including myself. I had good intentions; I just wanted to help someone, but I was not aware I also reacted to satisfy my own ego. I didn't know then that when you're playing a rescuer role, you can create victims; they remain helpless because you are finding a solution, not them.

Thankfully, now that I am more conscious of this rescuer tendency, I try to remember to ask first, "Would you like me to help you?"

If you said no, I'd accept and respect your decision. If instead you had said yes, my next question would be, "And what kind of help would you like?" That's the coach in me, using questions to get you to think more for yourself. You can learn to do this yourself, using Clean questions, which I'll tell you more about in chapter six.

APPLYING ALL THIS INFORMATION

When we are inhabiting our healthy self, we feel more integrated and at one with ourselves and regulate our emotions. We can become calmer and more grounded, think about what's going on and make deliberate decisions, and act intentionally. When I'm working as a coach, this is the state I aim to be in so I can best support clients to explore and find resources within themselves. One of my first priorities is to connect with the client in such a way as to settle their nervous system to help them to feel safe.

When one is feeling stressed, the nervous system is activated and can feel overwhelmed by demands and reality. With self-awareness, even in a state of stress, you can learn to self-regulate to help bring yourself back to a state of well-being.

Consider taking up practices like meditation, yoga, going for a walk, being in nature, or talking to a friend to relax and help regulate your nervous system. Chapter eleven will take a closer look at the healthy habits we can cultivate to keep us in a state of well-being more of the time and where we find the space to choose our response.

KEY MESSAGES

- Pay attention to the physiological sensations in your body more before interpreting what these sensations mean for you (e.g., my stomach is aching or tingling, my shoulders are heavy).

- When you notice yourself becoming uncomfortable, bring your attention to those sensations and take a conscious breath before doing anything else.

- When you become more conscious of what's going on inside your body and your mind, you can begin to create space, enabling you to move toward a calmer state. Only then will you access the higher-functioning part of your brain (the neo-cortex) and choose a response versus just reacting.

- Your turn. Think about times when you've felt stressed or overwhelmed. Ask yourself:

  - What happened, or what triggered, those feelings?

  - Is there a pattern to these times when I felt like that?

  - Do I have any concerning behaviors? If yes, what are they and how would I like to change?

  - Do I recognize what drama role I'm in when I'm not getting what I want? Persecutor, victim, or rescuer?

  - What would I like to have happen when I'm feeling stressed, or when I'm behaving in a drama role like that?

PART TWO

CHOICES

*The Koru symbol represents the young frond of the
silver fern, a native plant of New Zealand.*

It symbolizes life, growth, strength, and peace.

*Its shape conveys ideas of movement, latent and potential
energy, creation and renewal, light and enlightenment.*

CHAPTER 5

VALUING THE LIGHT

"Nothing can dim the light that shines from within."

MAYA ANGELOU

When we become more aware and appreciative of our light, or our strengths, we become more confident to trust ourselves. Marianne Williamson's poem, *Our Greatest Fear*, quickly became one of my personal favorites. It reminds me of that sense of inadequacy I have about myself; thoughts like "I'm not good enough" or "I'm not worthy." She indicates these may stem from some other underlying limiting belief we have about ourselves, or from trauma as discussed in chapter four.

This chapter takes a closer look at what a strength is and some of the choices we have in how we use our strengths. We also look at what our personal values are; the qualities and beliefs important to us. When we use strengths aligned to our values, we develop greater trust in ourselves.

PLAY TO YOUR STRENGTHS

You may have heard the saying "play to your strengths" as opposed to focusing on your weaknesses. But do you know what your strengths are? Do you know the full range of your strengths, not just the ones you use, but also the ones you are not using? Knowing what your strengths are is another fundamental building block to know thyself more, as well as being more intentional in choosing—even if the ability to choose may require development—which strengths to use and how much to use.

Much of my work as a coach is about helping clients to discover and develop their resources, one of which is their range of strengths. I believe we all have capacity for growth and development of our potential. That potential is like the potential contained in an acorn. Every acorn has a seed within containing the capacity for developing into a beautiful oak tree. How that seed actually grows and develops will depend on the quality of the soil, the amount of sunlight and water, the surrounding landscape, and time. How well we, as human beings, grow and develop depends on the environment we are nurtured in, the quality of relationships and experiences we have, and the decisions we make or don't make in our life.

I used to think a strength was "something you're good at." I've learned there's much more to understanding strengths than just that, and some things you might be good at are actually not strengths, but just learned behaviors which drain you. For example, I'm good at inputting data into a spread-sheet with great accuracy and speed, but I wouldn't call data entry an inherent strength of mine; it's simply a skill I needed to acquire and a task I needed to do as part of my role as an analyst, but I didn't feel energized after I inputted data apart from knowing that task was done.

Some years ago, a colleague asked me to try out a new psychometric questionnaire or tool called realise2. This questionnaire was developed by Dr. Alex Linley, the founding director of the Centre of Applied Positive Psychology at the

University of Leicester, and his team. realise2 aims to find out what your range of strengths is. Linley defined a strength in a particular way that goes way beyond just "what you're good at."

A strength is:

"a pre-existing capacity for a particular way of

behaving, thinking or feeling

that is authentic and energizing to the user,

and enables optimal functioning, development and performance."

Let's dissect Linley's definition and take a closer look at what it actually means:

- "A pre-existing capacity" means this capacity is innate. These capacities can be viewed as gifts you're born with. These gifts show themselves in one of three ways:

    a. The way we behave or act,

    b. In the way we think, or

    c. In the way we feel.

- "That is authentic and energizing to the user" means that, when we tap into our gifts and use them, somehow we feel more like the "real me"; we feel at ease with ourselves and are resourceful.

- "Enables optimal functioning, development and performance" means when we use our gifts, we work efficiently and effectively, becoming the best version of ourselves and achieve quality relationships and well-being.

REALIZED AND UNREALIZED STRENGTHS

One's strengths can be further classified as "realized" (they are being used) or "unrealized" (not being used for whatever reason). An unrealized strength might be because there is no awareness that one has this capacity or there hasn't been an opportunity to use or develop the capacity.

Linley also makes the distinction between a realized strength and a learned behavior. A learned behavior refers to skills we've developed to perform well, possibly because we had to do them as part of a job, but we don't get energized when we do it, like how I mentioned I'm good at data entry and administrative tasks. I had to do them, but I find doing them to drain my energy.

Furthermore, there is a fourth classification called "weaknesses" which are behaviors you're not good at doing *and* you find draining. For example, my husband has a weakness in making plans, especially plans for holidays. He's not good at that, lacking attention to detail about logistics and timing. I recognize his weakness in this area, and thus I do most of the planning, otherwise we'd never go on holiday together!

When you become clearer about what activities or tasks energize you, and what drains you, you can be more selective in what you decide to do. Be aware not to overuse a particular strength, as it can become a weakness. Instead, the advice is to:

- Use your realized strengths to best effect, but not too much, otherwise it can become a weakness.

- Find opportunities to use and develop unrealized strengths.

- Moderate your use of learned behaviors. Don't use them too much, otherwise you'll feel drained. Find someone who has a strength in this area and maybe suggest swapping tasks.

- Find ways to stop having to use your weaknesses.

APPLYING THE RESULTS

I couldn't wait to try out this realise2 strengths questionnaire. I wanted to know what my gifts, or strengths, are. My results were very interesting. I was amazed, shocked actually, to see my top unrealized strength was that of narrator or storyteller. My first thought was, "Hey, this can't be right!" and I started to have real doubts about the validity of this new tool. I knew I loved listening to stories, and storytelling was something I'd like to do well, but having tried a few times and, in my opinion, failing miserably, I stopped trying.

It wasn't until my fellow coach debriefed me about my results that we uncovered a big limiting belief living in my subconscious for decades. That limiting belief was "I'm no good at telling stories," and so I just stopped trying. Where did such a belief come from? I remembered a few instances where one or two people would comment, "Hurry up, Doris. What's your point?" or I'd be telling a story and then see someone's eyes glaze over, and that inner critic inside my head would confirm any doubts I'd have about my ability: "You're making a hash of this, so better stop."

Maybe the results of the questionnaire were valid. Maybe I did have an unrealized strength as a narrator. I decided there and then to try harder and develop this gift and move it from being unrealized to a realized strength. That's one of the reasons why I joined Epsom Speakers Club, a public speaking group part of Toastmasters International. I'm pleased to say my storytelling muscle is getting stronger every day.

I wonder what unopened gifts are sleeping inside of you, waiting to be woken up and developed. Think of the times when you've felt more yourself; more authentic and energized. Ask yourself, "What was I doing when I felt like that?" These are clues to your gifts. Don't make the mistake I made, judging my own level of competence as negative and not trying. With any skill, like an acorn, it takes time to flourish and bloom. It takes commitment, dedication, and persistence to improve.

I'll be discussing how you can apply your strengths more to get what you want in Part 3 of this book.

PERSONAL VALUES AND FINDING YOUR PATH
Strengths may be used in the pursuit of good objectives, like world peace, or bad objectives, like inciting violence or hatred. There is nothing implicit within a strength that determines it as good or bad. What's important in how you use your strengths is to be clear about the purpose or goal you hope to achieve, which leads me to look at what your personal values are. These are qualities and beliefs important to you.

Knowing what our personal values are can motivate us and guide our decisions. As you live by your values, they form the foundation for building greater trust in yourself.

Two values I hold dear are integrity and fairness. Integrity is about being honest and doing what you say you'll do. I believe it's important to say what I think and feel when it's appropriate. The reason I've qualified this with "when it's appropriate" is because in certain situations, it may "damage" you. I'm thinking of work situations where there is low psychological safety (see chapter eight for more about psychological safety).

In terms of fairness, I'm talking about equality: I treat people justly and without favoritism or discrimination. I expect others to do the same. When I see this isn't the case, which sadly is quite often, I've learned to speak up and voice my observations. I've become quite an activist for equality and inclusion and doing so makes me feel more in tune with who I am—the real me.

There's been quite a lot of research into strengths and personal values in the last two decades, primarily under the positive psychology movement. This began with Martin E. P. Seligman's American Psychological Association (APA) Presidential Address in 1998. Soon after, a scientific classification of twenty-four character strengths was developed and grouped under six headings. These character strengths are similar to personal values. Take a look at the box on the next page and see which character strengths resonate with you. This is a way of identifying your personal values. Then think about times in your life when these values supported your decisions in your work and life.

When we turn toward our light, we discover the direction and path we want to travel and make happen what we would like to have happen in our life. That's what the next chapters are about.

Character Strengths

Wisdom & Knowledge	Temperance	Transcendence
- Creativity - Curiosity - Open-minded-ness - Love of learning - Perspective	- Forgiveness and mercy - Humility - Prudence - Self-regulation or self-control	- Appreciation of beauty and excellence - Gratitude - Hope - Humor - Spirituality
Courage - Bravery - Persistence - Integrity - Vitality	**Humanity** - Love - Kindness - Social intelligence	**Justice** - Citizenship - Fairness - Leadership

KEY MESSAGES

- A strength is a way of behaving, thinking, or feeling that feels authentic and energizing for you. The more you use a strength, the better you get. But beware of overusing a strength, as it can become a weakness.

- Strengths take time to develop. You may have some unrealized strengths because you are unaware of them and/or you've not had any opportunity to develop them.

- Becoming more aware of your strengths and values enables you to make better decisions at work and in your life, and to remain true to your authentic self.

- Your turn. Here are some questions to help you identify your personal values. Get a blank sheet of paper and do a quick brainstorm, jotting down your answers. You can use your answers as a guide to figure out your personal values as you notice common words appearing:

  - What's important to you in life?

  - When you're reading or listening to news, what sort of story or behavior tends to inspire you?

  - What type of story or behavior makes you angry?

  - What do you want to change about the world or about yourself?

  - What are you most proud of?

  - When were you the happiest?

- Reflect on what strengths you have by thinking about what you've done or are doing:

  - What tasks or things do you like doing and feel energizing?

  - What haven't you tried that you'd like to?

CHAPTER 6

WHAT WOULD YOU LIKE TO HAVE HAPPEN?

"When the student is ready, the teacher will appear."

Lao Tzu, the ancient Chinese philosopher, wrote the above quote in the Tao Te Ching, the central text defining the philosophical basis of Taoism. I found this quote to be especially true when I discovered the magic of Clean Language, developed by pioneering psychotherapist and fellow New Zealander, David Grove.

Grove created a process called Clean Language when he was working with victims of trauma during the 1980s. He discovered they would often spontaneously describe their symptoms in metaphor. He found the most effective way of resolving a patient's traumatic memories was to honor their experience by repeating some of their exact words back to them. Grove also developed a series of simple questions with the least possible influence from the therapist. He called his process Clean Language, as the questions were "clean" in that they did not interfere with or contaminate their own experience. By using clean questions with his patients, Grove helped them work through their problems and blocks and foster the change they wanted.

While there are different levels of complexity to Clean Language, what I believe is most important is to appreciate the clean approach or philosophy which forms the foundation of Grove's creation. He was of Māori and European descent and took inspiration from his *whakapapa* and ancestral teaching (Goldsmith 2008). He maintained a healthy embryo is conceived as a *pristine being* with innate qualities and talents. A core belief is that people have a sense of the person they were born to be and there is a "life's path" they are meant to be on (Wilson 2017).

Unfortunately, life has a way of distorting and obscuring one's path, even in the womb (see chapter four about developmental trauma). Depending on what happens to people over time, incidents and experiences can create barriers obscuring some of our innate knowledge. Clean processes help to rediscover and reintegrate these lost pieces of knowledge, providing new energy and resources for the client.

I think it is this core belief that underpins Clean Language that sparked the touchstone in my psyche. I started training in Clean Language in 2017, and have since transformed my coaching practice and, in many ways, my life. In this chapter, I'll tell you about how I came to know about Clean and introduce you to some powerful and simple Clean Language questions which you can start using today.

COMING TO LEARN CLEAN

I first came across an article about Clean Language about ten years ago. I'd been working as an accredited executive coach with Ashridge Business School for several years by then. The main message I got from the article was about using the client's exact words instead of paraphrasing or summarizing what I had heard and understood, which I was quite skillful at doing.

What I hadn't realized was I was inadvertently influencing the client by doing so.

Even with just that small bit of insight from my reading, I changed the way I worked with my clients. I was amazed at how simply reflecting with a client's exact words or a selection of their words, without asking any questions at all, the client would open up and talk further about how they saw their situation. They seemed able to think further and deeper.

In 2017, I was surfing the internet and came across The Clean Coaching Centre, set up by Carol Wilson, an international performance coach and author. Wilson and Grove had collaborated to develop the application of Clean Language to coaching.

"David wanted to work with me because so many coaches were coming to his workshops. He wanted a course that would be safe for coaches who've had little training in therapy, unlike being a therapist or a psychiatrist where you have to be highly regulated," explained Wilson.

Wilson worked with Grove to develop courses aimed at using Clean Language specifically in coaching, and what is now known as Clean Coaching. This was the course I immediately enrolled in. Not only did I discover a wealth of information and processes to clean up my coaching practice, I met a wonderful community of fellow Clean advocates, practitioners, and learners from all over the world.

THE PROCESS OF CLEAN

At a simplistic level, Clean Language is a set of questions, or question structures, that make use of the exact words spoken, whether by a client, patient, student, friend, child, etc.

There are about twenty basic questions, but the two most used are: "What kind of X (is that X)?" and "Is there anything else about X?" The X represents the exact word or words spoken.

These two questions alone account for about 80 percent of responses from clients during a typical Clean Coaching session. Elements critical in the process include:

- Paying attention to someone

- Seeing them and hearing their words

- Repeating a selection of their exact words as input into a clean question.

In reflecting back on some of the exact words used, the speaker can hear themselves, and they have time to think further about what they've said. Furthermore, you refrain from making up your own interpretation of their words, which is what humans normally do. But the truth is, what a person means when they say a particular word can be quite different from what you mean when you use that same word.

Here's an example created by my Clean Coaching tutor, Angela Dunbar. Imagine your friend says he's "feeling a bit down," and you want to be as helpful as possible. What might you say?

- "Is it because your wife left you?" You may know his wife has left him, and thus this could be an obvious assumption and may be right; however, it does not encourage your friend to explore and draw upon his own knowledge and understanding, and could possibly upset him more because you reminded him of something he wasn't even thinking about at the moment.

• "What are you unhappy about?" This assumes "a bit down" equates to overall unhappiness for him. But how true is that? Do you know more than he does about his feelings?

• "How can you cheer yourself up?" This assumes cheering up is possible and is what he'd like as an outcome.

Now, imagine asking this instead: "And you're feeling a bit down. And when you're feeling a bit down, is there anything else about feeling a 'bit down'?"

The "is there anything else about 'feeling a bit down'" is a Clean question. Look carefully at the way the question is posed. Before asking the question, some or all his words are repeated and repeated again, but this time prefaced with "and when." This three-part syntax construction serves many purposes. The speaker:

• Hears their own words reflected back

• Feels listened to, understood, and not judged

• Has the opportunity to explore ideas and feelings before coming up with a solution

• Can take responsibility for deciding on their best course of action instead of relying on outside advice.

As a coach, I've found this technique works well. It frees up my having to do cognitive processing to work out what a client might mean, which is what I'd need to do if I was going to paraphrase or summarize. Instead, I can focus my attention on them and what they are expressing. At the heart of this process is attention— paying attention to someone and listening without judgment. This and unconditional positive regard will be elaborated on further in chapter eight. Paying exquisite attention is a skill anyone can learn.

USING CLEAN IN EVERYDAY CONVERSATION

You don't need to be a coach or a therapist to use Clean Language. Anyone can practice becoming a more attentive listener and less presumptive person and provide some space for inquiry or exploration in your everyday conversations.

Next time you are with a friend or colleague, focus on them and what they are saying *exactly*. When it's your turn to speak, identify something you'd like to find out more about regarding what they've said, and try asking one of the two common Clean questions from earlier.

Have a play with these examples of something your friend might say:

- "I've just had the most horrendous day."

- "I'm fine."

- "I'm so fed up."

- "That was just so out of this world!"

- "This is all so confusing. I don't know where to begin."

There's no one right answer. There are many different possible responses using either of those two Clean questions. Taking the first statement, you might reply with, "What kind of horrendous day is that?" or "Anything else about that horrendous day?"

You can also practice using Clean questions on yourself. I'd suggest you write down your responses so you can see your words in front of you; that's what I do when I use Clean questions as a self-inquiry process to help me think more thoroughly.

If I take that last sentence as an example, I could ask myself, "What kind of 'more thoroughly'?" and "Is there anything else about 'more thoroughly'?"

The idea is to have a go, try it out, and see what happens.

WHAT WOULD YOU LIKE...

Another very useful Clean question is, "What would you like to have happen?" When I first heard this question, it sounded strange. "To have happen" is not exactly common English parlance, but grammatically, it is correct. It places the emphasis on the future in terms of a desired (*what would you like*) outcome (*to have happen*). Some people may not even notice this somewhat peculiar phrasing. They hear it simply as a request to find out what they want; i.e., what is their goal.

Identifying what someone wants, their goal or their desired outcome, is a key first step in coaching. A commonly used framework is the GROW model (Whitmore 2009):

- Goal: what do you want?

- Reality: what is happening now?

- Options: what could you do?

- Will: what will you do?

I've found that for some people, they may not know what they want—they just know what they don't want or that they have a problem. When someone decides to come for coaching, the initial work is about identifying what the client would like to have happen. By exploring with them as cleanly as possible, how they got to where they are, they can identify more about the context of what they believe their problem or issue is. Then, when they narrow down this "problem" they don't want, they are able to articulate what they would like to have happen.

Other times, people may come to coaching because while they are 'doing well,' they wonder if there is something else out there they could be doing that might be more fulfilling or rewarding. They want to explore options with someone independent. If this is the case, being a Clean coach, some of the initial questions I might ask are, "What kind of 'fulfilling and rewarding' is that?" or "Is there anything else about 'fulfilling and rewarding'?" to encourage them to think more deeply about what they think they lack and want more of.

Once you are clearer about what you want to have happen, Clean coaches can then use Clean questions within the GROW framework to work with the client to come up with their own solutions.

Again, you don't have to be a coach to start using some of this information. The main point I would like you to take away is to focus on what you want as opposed to what you don't want. If that's difficult, think about what's working well now. Then think about what could be better—that's a reframing of "what's not working for you?"

MORE COMPLEX LEVELS

There is, of course, much more to Clean Language than a set of unbiased questions. There is a more systemic nature of the process to do with the way people often use metaphors when they speak. A metaphor is simply expressing one thing in terms of another.

In George Lakoff and Mark Johnson's groundbreaking book, *Metaphors We Live By*, these two linguists and philosophers highlight "that most of our ordinary conceptual system is metaphorical in nature" and they "...have found a way to begin to identify in detail just what the metaphors are that structure how we perceive, how we think, and what we do."

According to research studies, on average, we use about six metaphors a minute (Geary, 2011)—a fact I was quite surprised by.

To give you an idea of just how prevalent metaphors are in everyday language, look at the following statements where an argument is expressed in terms of war. Notice how the italicized words are used metaphorically (Lakoff and Johnson, 1980):

- He *attacked every weak point* in my argument.

- His criticisms were *right on target*.

- I *demolished* his argument.

- She *shot down* all his arguments.

Metaphors are like a container holding information at an unconscious level. David Grove discovered many of his trauma patients spoke in metaphor to describe their experiences. He found he could resolve traumatic memories by asking Clean questions directly of the metaphors. He did this in a strategically skillful way, which helped his patients to work through their problems and blockages, and to develop the change they wanted to have happen. I emphasized strategically skillful to show that while there is a simplistic level to Clean Language, there is a more complex level requiring time to learn, practice, and acquire.

THREE LEVELS OF THINKING

There are three different levels of thinking, or how we take in information:

- Sensing: by using our five senses (sight, smell, hearing, taste, and touch); this sense is "felt" in the body; an embodied sense of knowing.

- Conceptual: this is when we process what we've perceived via our senses and then infer or interpret a meaning to that feeling; "confident" is a concept, not a feeling. We can unpack the concept by asking a Clean question, like, "What kind of confident is that confident?" One might respond, "The kind of confident where I'm standing tall and feeling good about myself." Another person might respond differently: "The kind of confident where I'm not scared." The point is, concepts have different inferences for different people. Misunderstanding and miscommunication can easily happen if one assumes or presumes you know what the other means.

- Metaphoric: this is a more complex level of thinking and is expressed in metaphor. There is a literal meaning and a hidden or unconscious meaning in metaphors. For example: "I'm just hitting my head against a wall." This metaphor might indicate frustration, anger, hopelessness, or something else. Using Clean questions to inquire about the symbols contained in the metaphor directly produces information about the structure of thinking encapsulated within the metaphor, such as, "What kind of wall is that wall? What kind of hitting is that hitting? And is there anything else about all of that?"

EMERGENT KNOWLEDGE

After developing Clean Language, Grove went on to develop many other innovative processes using Clean Language. He learned not only do people carry information within the body, but they also carry it in the space around them as well. He developed a number of Emergent Knowledge (ΣK) processes based on the science of emergence and the theory of networks and systems as ways for someone to access information contained in those other spaces (Wilson 2017).

This ΣK concept fits into "knowing thyself," and thus trusting yourself more. Essentially, to get from where you are now to where you want to go, it's very likely the pathway or direction is not linear—otherwise you'd already be where you want to be, metaphorically speaking. The diagram on the next page illustrates, conceptually, what I mean by a non-linear approach.

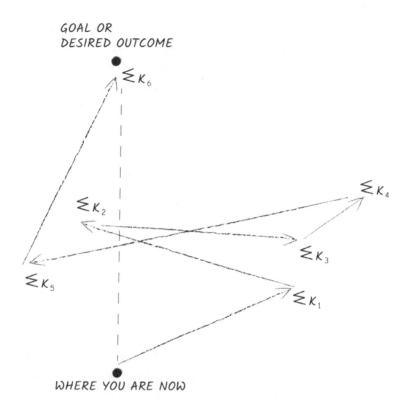

GOAL OR
DESIRED OUTCOME

ΣK_6

ΣK_2

ΣK_4

ΣK_3

ΣK_5

ΣK_1

WHERE YOU ARE NOW

Grove's ΣK experiments revealed that six was a magic number; 'magic' is my interpretation. When he asked a question six times, iteratively, new information or insight was gained. The first two or three times would often produce information one already knows. By the fourth iteration, there's likely to be a wobble in one's thinking—maybe frustration or annoyance. And, by the fifth and sixth iteration, something new or different arises. New information, new insights, and a different perspective on what's come up.

I use some of Grove's ΣK processes, like Clean Space and Clean Hieroglyphics, in my coaching practice, along with Clean

Language, with much success. Clients leave their sessions amazed at what they've learned about themselves.

A SACRED PRACTICE

The more I work with Clean practitioners and continue learning from them, I can appreciate Dr. Caitlin Walker's perspective of Clean as applied to groups, communities, and organizations.

"Clean Language is a sacred practice, sacred attention that celebrates humanity and the spark of life," she told me in an interview.

She went on to tell me about her early experience of working "cleanly" with difficult teenagers excluded from school, "These teenagers are the ones that everybody else would hate, they're horrible. But when you work with them cleanly, you see them in all their humanity. They reconnect with who they could have been, and should have been, and the bits of them that are still there, but hiding. Clean is really a sacred practice of being present to what is and trusting it."

Her words capture the spirit and approach to people and life which David Grove embodied in himself and in his work. There's something special at the heart of Clean beyond the usefulness of the technique with its various rules and methodology. Wilson summed it up like this:

> "Clean effortlessly passes through the noise of words, prejudices, fears, biases, and self-imposed limitations, allowing us to communicate directly with what David Grove called 'the pristine self': that essence of ourselves, uncontaminated by experience, which others have referred to as 'the real me,' 'intuition,' being 'in the zone,' or 'the unconscious mind'—that part of ourselves which always seems comfortable, which knows the way forward, where our energy is boundless, and where we can be at peace."

Perhaps that is why I resonated with Clean when I first read about it ten years ago. I've learned to trust myself and to follow that resonance within.

DAVID GROVE'S LEGACY

A principle Grove held dear was that his work was open source. "David's metaphor for himself was a launch pad for which others could lift off to discover new and unexplored worlds," explained psychotherapist and author James Lawley, who together with Penny Tompkins, has systematically documented Grove's work, as little of Grove's prodigious output existed in published form. Grove never trademarked or registered Clean Language or any of his wonderful innovations, and according to Lawley, "...his suggestion to his students was always to 'take my work and make it your own'" (Wilson 2017).

I believe it is this generosity of spirit that is alive in so many of the teachers and role models I've come across in my Clean journey. That journey led me to learn from and work with Clean enthusiasts all around the world, and this chapter is my small contribution to sharing their work.

While Clean Language can appear simple, it takes practice to apply. There are many layers. If you are intrigued and inspired by this little taste of Clean Language and Emergent Knowledge, I hope you'll look at the list of resources I've provided at the back of this book to learn more.

KEY MESSAGES

- Clean Language is a process to facilitate objective inquiry and collaboration. It requires you to pay attention to yourself and to others.

- Words have different meanings for different people. Using simple Clean questions can improve relationships by reducing miscommunication and misunderstanding.

- Your turn. Try using some simple Clean Language questions in everyday conversation:

    - Listen with care and attention to what someone is saying.

    - Recall a specific word or words they've actually said that you're curious to know more about.

    - Then simply ask, "What kind of X is that X?" (X being the word/s they used).

    - Then ask, "And is there anything else about X?"

    - Notice their reaction, facial expression, what happens, and what insights you can learn.

CHAPTER 7

RHYTHM OF TIME

"Grant me the serenity to accept the things I cannot change, the courage to change the things that I can, and the wisdom to know the difference."

These words were composed by the American theologian, Reinhold Niebuhr, and spread rapidly through Christian church groups in the 1930s and 1940s (Shapiro 2014). In 1955, these words became known as the Serenity Prayer when they appeared in publications of Alcoholics Anonymous (Sifton 2005). They form guiding principles adopted by Alcoholics Anonymous and other twelve step programs aimed at tackling problems, such as drug addictions and harmful compulsive behaviors. To me, they are great guiding principles underpinning the foundations for trusting yourself.

Serenity means "the state of being calm, peaceful, and untroubled," according to the Oxford Dictionary. As outlined in chapter four, when we're calm and aware of what's going on, we are likely to make better decisions about what to do, compared to when we're feeling frustrated, angry, or confused.

One thing we cannot change is time. There are only sixty minutes in an hour, twenty-four hours in a day, seven days in a week, and fifty-two weeks in a year. How you use those precious minutes and hours shapes who you become. Previous chapters explored the past—where you came from and where you've been to get you to where you are now.

This chapter takes a closer look at the concept of time and agency; the ability to be in control of oneself to decide or choose what you want to do, when, and for what purpose. When you have agency, you trust yourself more.

WHAT IS TIME?

Time is a concept or construct. This means it is no more than "an idea or theory containing various conceptual elements, typically subjective and not based on empirical evidence," according to the Oxford Dictionaries. Time is something we make up based on our experience of life and the habits we form around it.

According to neuroscientist David Eagleman, who researches the perception of time, there is actually no dedicated center of the brain for perceiving time and no sensory organ detecting the passing of time. He refers to the perception of time as "a distributed property of the brain that it is meta-sensory; it rides on top of all the others."

Different types of people think about time in different ways depending on how they perceive and experience it. In my facilitation work with groups, I've asked this Clean question: "For you, time is like what?" The question is seeking information about how one perceives time. The "...is like what?" is actually asking for a metaphor, although people will hear the question and respond in whatever way feels right for them.

Some people have said time is like a line, stretching out in front and behind them, or to the left and right of them. Some have said time is like a series of circles, spiraling in a loop. Others have said time is like a three-dimensional board game.

I wonder, for you, time is like what? There is no right or wrong answer. What's interesting is noticing what's similar and what's different between your own perception of time and that of others. Consider these other Clean questions to explore your sense of time more:

- When "time" is like that for you, where is your past?

- Where is your future?

- Where are you when time is like that?

Understanding more about your own and others' perception of time helps develop insights or ways of using time more effectively.

For me, time is like the *koru*, or a series of *koru* symbols spiraling from one cycle to the next, which I introduced earlier in the introduction to part two. The *koru* is a Māori symbol in the shape of a spiral or loop, resembling an unfurling sprout of the native New Zealand plant, the silver fern. The *koru* represents a symbol of survival and existence, of growth and development, as well as harmony and balance.

The spiraling nature of the *koru* symbol goes on infinitely for me, as if there is no beginning nor end. In practical terms, I view my past as being behind me, to my left side, while my future is forward to my right. I feel as if my present is where I am now, and my past and future are integrated within where I am now. That integration is the sense of knowing where I've been and where I want to go. When time is like that, I have a sense of autonomy and agency; I am my own person and I can choose what to do with my life. I feel free.

THE SPEED OF TIME

On a cognitive level, I am acutely aware time is marching on, at a regular pace, second by second, and minute by minute. You just look at the clock to know this. But when I'm doing something I'm fully engaged in, time can feel like it's moving fast. Other times, like when I'm at a meeting that's rather dull and boring, time moves at a snail's pace.

Thus, there is an emotional level to the construct of time. Given what we know about what's going on inside (see chapter four), and how our brains and neurology work, we need to be in a calmer, more mindful state in order to access our neocortex to make considered responses and decisions about what you want.

One's sense of time passing is closely linked to the amount of memory the brain lays down. Time spent in new places or situations requires us to notice a lot of detail and seems to last longer because we are laying down more memories. Compare that to when you are scrolling through the internet and time seems to fly by if you don't pay attention (Stuart Smith, 2021).

AUTOBIOGRAPHICAL TIMELINE

One's autobiographical timeline is composed of one's memories. As Stuart Smith, psychiatrist and author of *The Well-Gardened*

Mind: Rediscovering Nature in the Modern World, pointed out: "Memories have a much stronger relationship to place or location, than chronological passing of time." In other words, *where* something happened is more memorable than *when* it happened.

There is an evolutionary reason for this. Our ancestors, who used to live in the wild, needed a map of the terrain and remembering where resources were mattered for survival. Location or place functions like an index card in the memory system. Therefore, places become intimately associated with our autobiographical story, and our sense of self. That's why it's important to ask yourself the question posed in chapter two: "Where do you come from?"

Places or locations, like where you were born and grew up, or where you went to school, contain information about your past— people you were with and what happened there that helped shape you. Those places and pieces of information are glued to your memory, and you'll remember who you were and how you came to be where you are now.

LIVING IN THE NOW

As humans, we can live in the present, dwell on the past, and project into the future. But while we *can,* it doesn't mean we *do.* Some people may feel stuck in the past and have anxieties about the future, making it difficult to focus on the here and now. This may be a result of past experiences leaving "wounds" or trauma on one's psyche (see chapter four for more about this).

Gardening and nature can be brilliant partners to help restore oneself and heal the human condition. "There is no negotiating with the march of the seasons, or the pace of the natural growth force. You cannot slow them down or speed them up. You have to submit to the rhythm of garden time. And you have to work within that frame," said Stuart Smith.

There are times when the rolling sequence of tasks to maintain a garden can become too much and you get tired and worn out. Submitting to the rhythm of "garden time," as Smith called it, is having the serenity to accept these things you cannot change. Instead, it is you who needs to slow down.

Being in nature can bring us back to the basic biological rhythms of life. When you're in a garden, the pace of life is the pace of plants. While I didn't much appreciate working in our family's market garden as a kid, how I've changed my mind as I get older. I now enjoy being in my garden, digging up the weeds, planting spring bulbs, pruning the climbing rose bush, and being careful not to let the thorns prick me. Many people have found gardening as one activity that helps them slow down and shift to a more reflective state of mind.

Simply being in nature, whether going for a walk or a leisurely bike ride, also allows you to slow down. Contrast this slower, more reflective pace with today's world of fast food, speed dating, one-click ordering, same-day delivery, endless stream of posts, notifications, emails, and tweets, etc. There's so much going on and new information and it's hard to know what's relevant. There is a lack of time to digest experiences, understand, or even remember it for oneself.

PAUSE AND CHECK IN

It is vital to pause, to have space and time to digest, physically and mentally, to find and make meaning. Just as our physiological bodies need time to rest and digest food, we also need time to metabolize our sensations, feelings, and emotions.

How well can you balance your time between work, rest, and play?

Finding or allocating time to "slow down, pause, and reflect" is particularly important in times of high stress and uncertainty. During the first wave of COVID-19 in 2020, hospitals were overwhelmed with patients needing intensive care. During the past eighteen months, I have facilitated several group sessions with various National Health Service staff teams as my way of giving back to the health service. These were a series of one-hour sessions held online. For staff who attended, it was reassuring to hear how much they valued the opportunity to pause from their unrelenting schedules and check in with each other and themselves. In expressing what's been going on for them and hearing others' experiences, staff realized they shared many similar stories. "We left these sessions feeling re-energized and closer as a team," reported one team leader.

RISK OF BURNOUT

Pausing is important because if you don't have enough time to rest and recover, you are at risk of burnout. Burnout refers to the physical or mental collapse caused by overwork or stress (Freudenberger 1974). Burnout tends to be a function of chronic work stress and disengagement. It is what happens when there's not enough recovery time and the ability to regulate stress is lost. Thus, the risk of depression and other disorders, including heart disease and diabetes, increases.

The Swedish University of Agricultural Sciences developed an intensive twelve-week program of garden therapy specifically for treating burnout and stress in their "living lab" called the Alnarp Rehabilitation Garden.

Most of the patients at Alnarp are high-achieving, conscientious women from stressful industries such as teaching, nursing, medicine, and law. Through overload of work and family commitments, they suffer from anxiety and lack mental and physical energy, finding it hard to concentrate or make decisions. Furthermore, because their self-esteem is strongly invested in performing well at their job, they struggle with feelings of guilt and shame about being off work. They are disconnected from their bodies and the world (Stuart-Smith 2021).

Part of their disconnection is because they have long since stopped listening to warning signals indicative of burnout, such as:

- Chronic low energy and exhaustion.

- When small issues produce a strong emotional reaction.

- Getting sick more often as the immune system breaks down.

- Having a sense of inefficacy, i.e., feeling like you can't produce results in your life. When you lose efficacy, your confidence plummets, you feel less effective at work, and it impact your self-worth.

- Feeling disengaged from those things that usually give you energy and enthusiasm at work.

Burned-out professionals report lack of attention and other cognitive failures, such as saying things you might regret, forgetting names, or missing important cues in the environment, like a stop sign while driving (Aydemir 2013).

The repetitive garden activities and tasks at Alnarp allowed participants to find a sense of rhythm. And that sense of rhythm when the mind, body, and environment came together in harmony brought meaning back to their lives. By being in nature and working in the garden, the women were able to reconnect at the most basic level, through their senses and feelings. Being in touch with nature helped them become more in touch with themselves (Stuart-Smith 2020).

It's also critical to get enough quality sleep for your longer-term well-being. According to Stuart Smith, "...sleep is when the microglia cells in the brain carry out their restorative pruning and weeding activities, but many people run short on this most basic form of rest and recovery time."

TIME WITH NATURE HEALS

The natural environment, with its trees, stones, flowers, and water—all part of the intentional design of Alnarp Rehabilitation Garden—is in contrast to today's environment where technology often interferes with people's ability to relate to nature.

According to American psychiatrist and psychoanalyst Harold Searles, "Over the decades, we have come from dwelling in another world in which the living works of nature, either predominated or were near at hand to dwelling in an environment, dominated by technology, which is wonderfully powerful, and yet, nevertheless, dead."

The garden therapy, alongside just being in the natural environment, gave those burned-out women time and space to reconnect with themselves. In-depth interviews with participants, both during and three months after attending Alnarp, revealed the unconditional acceptance of nature was therapeutically important to them (Stuart-Smith 2020). The feeling of safety enabled them to experience and release their emotional distress. Through spending time close to nature, they learned there is a time for everything.

KEY MESSAGES

- Time is a construct. You cannot save time or store it. You can't control time, but you can decide how you use it and for what purpose.

- Learning to use your time wisely and effectively requires you to make choices of what to do when.

- Maintaining a healthy balance of time for work, rest, and play enables you to have greater agency: the feeling of being in control of your life.

- Your turn. Take a look at how you spend your time in a day and over a week.

    - Identify how much time is for work, for rest, for play.

    - Is the balance right?

    - What needs to happen for you to get rest and recover throughout your day?

PART THREE

BEHAVE

The yin-yang is a Taoist symbol, representing the idea that two opposite characteristics can exist in harmony and complement each other. There can be no light without darkness.

The smaller circles nested within each half of the symbol serves as a reminder of the interdependent nature of opposites.

All relative existence is in constant flux and change, appearing and dissolving continuously, as the elements of which they are composed go through their birth-and-death cycles.

CHAPTER 8

LEARNING TO LEARN

"That is what learning is. You suddenly understand something you've understood all your life, but in a new way."

DORIS LESSING

In chapter one, I outlined my 4C model of trust: consistency, compassion, competence, and communication, with communication being the glue connecting the other three components. Learning to cultivate trust in yourself and with others is about developing competence and confidence, while communicating effectively is about listening and speaking; listening deeply to what is said and listening to the silence between the gaps of words, and speaking is about being heard and understood. Both listening and speaking are skills.

In this chapter, we'll start by looking at a general model of learning applicable to learning any skill. Becoming more aware about the process of learning and becoming more skillful in whatever you are trying to perfect builds confidence in your abilities. This in turn enables you to trust yourself more. When you exude greater self-confidence, others will feel greater trust in you as well.

Then, I want to focus on the kind of attention paving the way for connection with others, and what leads to compassionate communications. We'll consider some specifics of effective listening and speaking, including the giving and receiving of feedback.

CONSCIOUS COMPETENCE

Like any skill, it takes time and practice to achieve a desired level of performance. Expect to feel uncomfortable at first, especially when your level of competence is low. But let me reassure you, feeling uncomfortable means you're at the edge of your level of competence or comfort zone. With practice and persistence, you'll move on.

A useful model of learning is the conscious competence model. It takes you from an initial incompetent stage to a competent one, via levels of consciousness (Broadwell 1969).

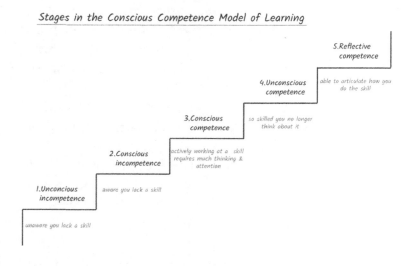

Stages in the Conscious Competence Model of Learning

5.Reflective competence — able to articulate how you do the skill

4.Unconscious competence — so skilled you no longer think about it

3.Conscious competence — actively working at a skill requires much thinking & attention

2.Conscious incompetence — aware you lack a skill

1.Unconcious incompetence — unaware you lack a skill

Like any model, it's a simplified way to understand more complex processes. I like this model because it highlights the need to be aware first, and how levels of competence are a function of practice plus underlying capabilities; that is, some people may have some innate strengths enabling them to pick up the skill much faster (see chapter five for more about strengths). For example, if you've grown up playing tennis or hockey, you'll probably become quite competent relatively quickly in, say, golf, compared to someone who has never played a sport involving hitting a ball.

In the original model, there is only the first four stages. There is possibly a fifth stage of learning. For some, reaching the fourth stage—where doing the skill is instinctive—means they may become unaware of how they are doing it. But there may be others able to reflect on their competence level and articulate "how."

This fifth stage was proposed in 2004 by higher education consultant David Baume, who called it "reflective competence." He said, "If unconscious competence is the top level, how on earth can I teach things I'm unconsciously competent at...so, reflective competence—a step beyond unconscious competence" (Baume, 2004).

CULTIVATING UNCONDITIONAL POSITIVE REGARD

My innate curiosity means I love learning and the process of learning to learn. I enjoy application to different contexts. That's why I decided to transition from being an economist, to teaching business development and strategy, to becoming a coach. I also wanted a more flexible lifestyle, more autonomy about when to work, and where I could work with individuals to support their growth and development.

As part of my training to be a coach, I learned about Carl Rogers, an eminent American psychologist, and his approach to therapy called "unconditional positive regard." Rogers, together with Abraham Maslow, who developed the hierarchical theory of human motivation and needs, are the founding fathers of humanistic psychology which took root in the late 1950s and early 1960s. This approach emphasized looking at the whole person and the uniqueness of each individual, with the assumption people have free will and are motivated to achieve their potential and self-actualize (McLeod 2015).

Those three words, unconditional positive regard, resonated with me and I had an intuitive sense of their meaning. It is about accepting a person "without negative judgment of... [a person's] basic worth" (Rogers 1980).

This made sense to me as a coach, where the underlying assumption common in coaching philosophy and approach is the client is resourceful, despite whatever negative thoughts, problems, or situations they may have (this is akin to the "healthy self" concept as discussed in chapter four). As a coach, my job is to work with the client to uncover and discover those resources that will energize, enable, and empower them to achieve what they would like to have happen.

It did take some time, however, for me to learn how to put unconditional positive regard into practice and become "unconsciously competent." While I was aware of the concept, I didn't really know how to do it in practice. I had to learn more about empathy and compassion, how to convey these feelings to another, as well as how to embody such feelings, and do it with authenticity.

WHAT IS EMPATHY?
According to the Online Etymology Dictionary, "empathy" comes from Greek and means to be "in feeling." The word "compassion" comes from Latin and means "to suffer with."

For me, empathy is sensing within my own body what the other person is feeling, whereas compassion is the translation of that empathy from my body to my mind, making it a conscious response to be in relation with another, however alienating or distressing those feelings may be.

I only really appreciated this distinction after my own experience of suffering during my clinical depression in my forties. Part of my recovery was to become more compassionate to myself first. That involved having to accept all the many parts of myself—the good, the not-so-good, and the bits I wanted to change.

I came to learn more about Rogers' approach to therapy from reading the best-selling book, *Kitchen Table Wisdom—Stories That Heal* by Dr. Rachel Naomi Remen. Remen was an early pioneer of holistic and integrative medicine, a member of the Stanford University School of Medicine faculty, and often sought for her expert opinion. She, along with a small group of traditional physicians and psychologists, was invited to attend a day-long master's class with Dr. Carl Rogers. It was the first time she'd met Rogers, and her initial perceptions of him surprised her.

To her, his style was very different from the articulate and authoritative presentation style she was accustomed to at the medical center. Rogers paused often to put into words what he was doing. In her book, Remen recalled her thoughts about Rogers and his approach: "Could someone so seemingly hesitant have any expertise at all? I doubted it. From what I could gather, unconditional positive regard came down to sitting in silence and accepting everything the patient said without judgment or interpretation. I could not imagine how this might prove helpful."

I love her honesty in expressing exactly what she thought at the time. Her beautiful description of Rogers' live session with a volunteer stood out to me. Rogers didn't say a single word, yet he conveyed a total acceptance of the volunteer, a doctor, exactly as he was, simply by the quality of his attention (Remen, 2006).

"In the safe climate of Rogers' total acceptance, [the doctor] began to shed his mask, hesitantly at first and then more and more easily," recalled Remen. "As each mask fell, Rogers welcomed the one behind it unconditionally, until finally we glimpsed the beauty of the doctor's naked face. I doubt that even he himself had ever seen it before."

From Remen's description and my knowledge of Rogers' work from his book, *A Way of Being*, a collection of his professional and personal development from the 1960s to the eighties, I recognized what I had to work on to develop more unconditional positive regard:

- Exquisite attention and deep listening

- Acceptance without judgment of the other

- Compassion for myself and the other

Much of my development as a coach, and as a human being, has been about developing and honing these skills, or capacities, for empathy and compassion. When these capacities become an innate part of who we are, and who we want to become, we learn to trust ourselves and others more.

BELIEVING IN HUMANITY
A skill is a learned ability to do something well, and to that extent, you can learn how to be more compassionate, to listen more deeply, and be less judgmental about people.

But to do these well, so well they become an innate part of who you are, you have to believe; believe in the inherent value of these human qualities. These are the kinds of beliefs and qualities underpinning David Grove's Clean approach (see chapter six) and which I have come to appreciate and value so much.

In her book, Remen mentioned the safe climate created by Carl Rogers' total acceptance of the volunteer in his demonstration. When you know and feel you are totally accepted without judgment, you can take off your mask and relax and speak freely. The condition of safety which was evident in Rogers' demonstration is equivalent to what is now termed "psychological safety," a concept popularized by Harvard Business School professor Dr. Amy Edmondson in 1999.

PSYCHOLOGICAL SAFETY

Edmondson studied clinical teams and the number of mistakes each team made when she was surprised to find the teams with a higher number of good outcomes made more mistakes than teams with fewer good outcomes. Her further investigations discovered, in fact, the teams with better outcomes were admitting more mistakes, while the teams with fewer good outcomes were more likely to hide their mistakes (Edmondson 2019).

Underpinning psychological safety is trust; trust that it's safe to be yourself and say what is on your mind without fear. If you don't feel safe, you are less likely to speak up, contribute ideas, or admit to mistakes.

Given today's volatile, uncertain, complex, and ambiguous (VUCA) world, the style of leadership required in many companies and organizations is one of collaboration. Leaders need to create conditions for psychological safety so a diverse range of thinkers and contributors can speak and be heard without fear of being punished or humiliated. This requires developing trusting relationships so people from all levels contribute ideas openly.

The concept of psychological safety applies in all areas of work and life. Think about yourself as a member of a sports team, a business team, or any other group of individuals with a shared goal. How good did it feel being a member? Are you able to be yourself, ask for help, free to admit mistakes, and challenge ideas without fear of humiliation or embarrassment?

COURAGE TO SPEAK UP

Teaching yourself to speak up also takes courage, vulnerability, and practice. It's also a skill, and one I've been working on most of my life. The turning point for me was in 2006, when I experienced speaking more from my heart rather than from my head.

I was attending the third day of a three-day workshop about ontological (the nature of being human) coaching. During the afternoon coffee break, I was with a group of people making some rather derogatory comments about two participants, Susan and Jane, saying how they viewed their input as "showing off, too eloquent, and always had something to say."

I listened in amazement. Their perception of these women's behavior was so different from my own. From my perspective, these two women represented boldness and courage for being able to speak with such passion from their hearts so easily. They eagerly shared their thoughts and feelings without, what seemed to me, any care in the world of what others would think of them.

I told a friend who was part of the delivery team how wonderful I thought Susan and Jane were and how some others were so negative about them. She encouraged me to tell the two women directly what I thought about them, assuring me they would appreciate hearing it. But I didn't have time to do that as the coffee break ended and we all reconvened in the meeting room.

"Does anyone have anything to share?" asked the workshop leader.

This was the usual question posed after coffee breaks. Somehow, I found myself raising my hand—the first time I'd done so during the whole three-day workshop. I stood up and somehow, in a shaky voice, said how much I appreciated the contributions of these two women and how impressed I was with their boldness and passion. I said they had qualities which I'd like to have more of, and I was aware other people might have different perceptions of them, that their forthright expressions could be interpreted as being arrogant or a desire to "hog the space"; at least, I think I included that bit too.

When I looked over at where Susan and Jane sat, I noticed tears in their eyes. They both mouthed "thank you" to me. I quickly sat down. I was still a bit shaky as I was not used to speaking up. But I also felt relieved and pleased I'd said what I thought and felt.

But then the workshop leader asked me to come up to the front of the room.

Oh no, why? What on Earth does he want me to do? was the immediate panicked thought that crossed my mind. All eyes were on me as I stood up hesitantly and walked to the front.

He asked me to stand and look out at everyone sitting in the room. Silence. I turned and looked out at the sea of faces in the audience. Their eyes were all fixed on me. Those few seconds felt like an eternity.

"Tell me, what do you see?" the workshop leader asked.

I swallowed. Apart from giving a literal description of everyone's faces, I said I didn't know. Then, after a moment, I added, "I see more, but I don't know what more."

It seemed as if the sunlight streaming into the room had suddenly gotten brighter. And then I saw, or more accurately, I *felt*, those many faces and eyes looking back at me. I felt as if I could see into these people's souls and feel what they felt inside. Love. Gratitude. Admiration. Hope.

I can't quite find the words to express what I was feeling. All I know is that by speaking up and vouching for Susan and Jane, I had this awesome, amazing, absolutely incredible experience. Now, whenever I practice empathy and compassion, whether with myself, my family, friends, colleagues, or my coaching clients, my neurology and body remember that feeling and I find it easier to speak from my heart.

FEEDBACK BUILDS TRUST

About ten years ago, I decided to join a public speaking club, part of the global Toastmasters International network. It's a friendly and supportive community, where we encourage each other with commendations, recommendations, and constructive feedback. It's a safe place to practice public speaking, make mistakes, and learn to get better.

Outside this club setting, the skill of giving and receiving feedback is also a valuable life skill for work and home. It's useful to distinguish between three different kinds of feedback, particularly for work purposes (Hudson, 2021).

- Appreciation: positive comments or praise, letting people know what you want them to keep doing, or to do more often because they are doing it well.

- Coaching: helping someone figure out how to do something, not by telling them how you would go about doing it, but by asking questions. Start by asking questions to find out what they already know. They may be unaware of something you know, so inform them about that. Then, with this added information, ask them further questions about what they could do now about their issue or problem. Be patient and allow space for them to respond.

- Evaluation: this kind of feedback is when someone wants to know where they stand. Are they in line for a promotion? A pay raise? Are they where they should be in terms of their length of time in the role? Are they meeting your expectations? If they want to know this kind of information, and you feel it is appropriate to inform them of your assessment, then do so.

If you're asked to give someone feedback, don't assume you know what kind of feedback they want. Invite them to be more specific about what they would like. When you are giving an evaluation type of feedback, it is often better to combine it with a coaching conversation.

Therese Hudson, author of *Let's Talk: Make Effective Feedback Your Superpower*, provides an example of how to do this well: "I'd love to give you some feedback. What would be most helpful to you right now? Do you want me to let you know what I love about your work? Would you like some coaching and advice, or do you want to know where you stand?"

By asking these types of questions, it allows the person seeking feedback to think further about what they really want. And thus, there is no need for the manager to assume anything.

These three kinds of feedback don't need to be separate conversations. In fact, aim to give a lot more appreciation than the other two types of feedback. That builds trust between the both of you and trust within the person that they can do the job well.

BE APPRECIATIVE AND SPECIFIC

What's important is to be specific about what it is someone is doing that you appreciate. Too often, I hear people offering positive feedback or praise in generalized terms: "Well done, I'm so pleased for you" or "That was an amazing job you did" or "That was awesome."

When someone says these positive things to you, it may give you a warm feeling at first, but it would be even better if they told you what exactly you did that was so amazing or awesome.

Most people are not good at giving feedback, let alone specific feedback. It's a skill, and everyone can learn how to be better. As someone receiving feedback, you can play a role to help the feedback-giver by acknowledging their feedback *and* by asking for some more specific information: "Thank you. What in particular are you so pleased about with me?" or "Thank you. What did I do that was so amazing?" or "Thanks. What specifically did I do that was so awesome?"

This shows you are:

1. Listening

2. Showing appreciation about what they have said to you ("thank you")

3. Building understanding by engaging with what they have said by inquiring further.

Asking for feedback is an indication that there is some level of trust in the relationship. If you are asked to give someone feedback, asking them what they'd like specifically is another step toward building the relationship and building trust overall.

KEY MESSAGES

- We all have our own preferred way of learning, but there are certain stages we all go through to learn a new skill. We might begin at a very low level of competence simply because we don't know how to do it.

- With time, practice, and feedback, we get better.

- Belief in your own conviction and commitment is important. Trust yourself to make a commitment with yourself. Honor that commitment, just as you would honor one with a friend.

- Your turn. Ask yourself, "When I'm learning at my best, that's like what?" Jot down all the things that spring to mind. Consider these aspects:

  - What kind of environment suits you best?

  - When is the best time of day or night for learning for you?

  - What kind of support would help you with your learning?

  - How are you feeling when you're learning at your best?

- Try speaking up more often, especially when you notice people (friends, family members, direct reports, colleagues, bosses, etc.) are doing things well.

  - Offer appreciative feedback more often. You'll build more trust with them and a better relationship.

CHAPTER 9

COMPASSION IS CARING

"People at birth are inherently good."

At the heart of cultivating trust in ourselves and others is our capacity for compassion and our ability to communicate with compassion. In her acceptance speech for winning Best Director in the 2021 Oscar awards for *Nomadland* (which also won Best Picture), Chloé Zhao cited what she learned when she was a kid growing up in China, and how she kept going when things got hard:

> "[M]y Dad and I used to play this game. We would memorize classic Chinese poems and texts, and we would recite them together and try to finish each other's sentences. There's one I remember so dearly, it's called the Three Character Classics. The first phrase goes...'People at birth are inherently good.' Those six letters had such a great impact on me when I was a kid, and I still truly believe them today."

I also believe people are born good, even though sometimes it might seem like the opposite is true. Unlike Zhao, this wasn't a belief I've had since I was a kid. Back then, I had many beliefs about just how bad I was and how bad other people could be when things didn't go well, like how I used to look down on mental illness and think being vulnerable was a sign of weakness. I was full of judgments about myself and others, opinions I'd keep to myself as I was also ashamed to admit them. In many ways, this explains why I was so hesitant in voicing my opinions and speaking up as a kid. Despite my outward confident appearance, I often felt unsure of myself.

Thankfully, I now appreciate the value of being less judgmental and more open-minded, as well as learning how to be more compassionate, especially to myself. I know now people's behaviors are not necessarily expressions of who they are at their core. Poor or bad behavior could simply be a byproduct of how they've grown up, the conditions they've experienced, or their habitual "reactions" to stimuli pushing their buttons (see chapter four for more information). I remember when I was not that generous in assigning such probable causes to what I judged to be behavior fueled from, in my opinion, malevolent intent.

This chapter builds on the last one and explores ways to communicate more effectively and with compassion, beginning with a personal story.

ARMORING UP

When I was in my mid-thirties, I transitioned my career from an economist to a lecturer and tutor in executive education. I was relatively new in the role, but received supportive and encouraging reviews from participants and colleagues. Then one day, I was called in to see the director of Human Resources. His secretary said she'd no idea what it was about. I knocked on his door and went in. I was surprised to see my immediate boss also in the room. They proceeded to tell me my performance was not good enough and I should consider resigning.

Immediately, my sympathetic nervous system kicked in and my whole body tensed up; I sensed danger. I wanted to break down and cry, but there was no way I would show those two powerful men with managerial authority my true feelings. I didn't trust them one iota, especially in that moment. This was the first time I'd heard that I wasn't doing a good job. I knew enough about HR disciplinary procedures to know what they were suggesting didn't meet standard protocol.

My "surviving self" (see chapter four) put on her armor. I swallowed hard, took in a deep breath, and proceeded to interrogate both men, asking for specific evidence to support their allegations of my poor performance. I wrote down every single word they uttered. I collected my own evidence of their accusations.

I knew I needed time to reflect and talk to people I trusted about what was happening. I found out later that other faculty staff had been subjected to this type of, what felt like, bullying behavior from these two men before.

So what happened? I didn't resign. Instead, I told them if my performance was not up to standard, they needed to give me development opportunities to improve, as per the protocol according to the Staff Handbook. I'm pleased to say I ended up attending a wonderful international teachers' program, fully funded by the organization. This helped to not only develop my competence and confidence as a teacher, but also connected me with fellow teachers from across the globe.

Because I choose to believe people are inherently good, I gave those two powerful men the benefit of the doubt. Perhaps they weren't just nonsensical bullies who felt threatened; perhaps they were just very poor at giving feedback and lacking in people management skills. With time and practice, and a little more compassion, I hope, should there be a next time they call an employee into their office, they do so with more care. Fortunately, I trusted myself and my abilities enough to know these two men were incorrect in their judgments of me, and because of that trust, I gained so much more.

COMMUNICATING WITH COMPASSION

Too often when we communicate with others, irrational conflicts and misunderstandings arise and we end up leaving conversations feeling disregarded, in despair, or disgruntled. In his book *Nonviolent Communication*, American psychologist Marshall Rosenberg shares a way of communicating that helps build healthy relationships because it helps people understand each other better.

When I first read his term, "nonviolent communications," I was put off investigating further. I inferred that non-violence had something to do with violence like fighting and war. It does, but not in the way I thought. As the book explained:

> "If "violent" means acting in ways that result in hurt or harm, then much of how we communicate—judging others, bullying, having racial bias, blaming, finger pointing, discriminating, speaking without listening, criticizing others or ourselves, name-calling, reacting when angry, using political rhetoric, being defensive or judging what's "good/bad" or what's "right/wrong" with people—could indeed be called "violent communications.""

According to Rosenburg's definition, "nonviolent communications is a way of communicating that leads us to give from the heart." His purpose with nonviolent communication is to help us connect with ourselves and others in a way that makes us express ourselves more compassionately. It is not about convincing people to do what we want, but creating a connection with another person where everyone's needs are met and we can resolve differences peacefully.

When someone says, "You never listen to me!" in an angry tone, what do you think is going on? What they have said, and how they have said it, is in fact a judgment, a criticism, and an interpretation of the other person. It's likely the recipient of this message might react defensively and/or counterattack, instead of trying to understand what's going on. If the speaker is angry, *why* are they angry? Surely that's the real issue.

But we won't get to know the real issue if the communication remains violent, like this attacking and defensive exchange of words. As Rosenburg pointed out, when we make judgments, criticisms, and interpretations of others, we imply the person in front of us is wrong or behaving wrongly. Instead, his nonviolent communications process is aimed at recognizing what unmet need we have and finding a way to express it so others can understand us more with greater compassion.

Just as Chloé Zhao and myself believe people are born inherently good, so does Rosenburg: "[I]t is our nature to enjoy giving and receiving in a compassionate manner." At the core of nonviolent communication is the belief that all human beings have the capacity for compassion and empathy (Rosenburg 2015).

EMPATHETIC CONCERN

When you are authentically compassionate, you need to really care about the other. That's what empathetic concern is about. This is a higher level of empathy that builds on:

1. Cognitive empathy, where you have an understanding about how you see things and how you think about the world.

2. Emotional empathy, where you know or are aware of what you feel and the other person's feelings too (Goleman 2006).

To quote Daniel Goleman, psychologist and author of *Emotional Intelligence*, "There is no compassion without caring." Really caring about what's in the best interest of someone is fundamental in developing compassion. Research studies show the kind of leaders people love to work for are those who can be tough when they need to be, but also care about you and have your back (Goleman 2006).

Caring and compassion are on a continuum together. At one end, there is no or little care for another; one might just be self-absorbed and only care about themselves, therefore with no compassion. The more you care about another, the more compassionate you will be.

Care and Compassion Continuum

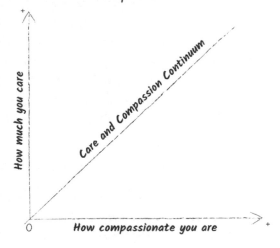

Building your empathetic concern muscle is about developing emotional intelligence (EQ), defined as "the ability to perceive, use, understand, manage, and handle emotions." The higher your EQ, the more you recognize your own emotions and those of others (Goleman 2008).

Unlike your IQ or cognitive abilities, which are basically hardwired and don't really change much through life, your EQ is learned and learnable, and you can upgrade it at any point (Goleman 2020). That's good news, and chimes with Rosenburg's belief that all humans have the capacity for compassion, and his book is a big step toward developing that capacity.

NONVIOLENT COMMUNICATION (NVC)

Thinking back to when I was young, I often made judgments about people. If I didn't like or understand someone, I'd react in terms of what I saw as their wrongness. For example, when a driver pulled out in front of me in traffic, I'd tend to react with, "You stupid idiot!" If a teacher asked me to do something I didn't want to do, they were mean and picking on me. If my work colleague wanted more details, I'd think they were picky and missing the big picture. On the other hand, if I wanted more details than they gave, they were sloppy and disorganized. If my partner wanted more attention or affection than I gave him, he was needy and dependent, but if I wanted more attention and affection from *him*, then he was insensitive and uncaring.

I realize now, having understood Rosenburg's principles behind NVC, "we all pay dearly when people respond to our values and needs not out of a desire to give from the heart, but out of fear, guilt or shame" (Rosenburg 2019).

He pointed out, sooner or later, we'll experience a loss of goodwill if people feel they are complying with us out of a sense of coercion. This damages trust and relationships. When people respond out of fear, guilt, or shame, they are likely to feel resentment and decreased self-esteem, which in turn can reduce their trust in themselves and others.

It's important to distinguish between value judgments and moralistic judgements. We all make value judgments: these reflect our beliefs about what we value in life, such as qualities like honesty, freedom, and peace. On the other hand, we might make moralistic judgments of people and behaviors that don't support or align with our value judgments.

Take, for example, "Violence is bad and people who kill others are evil." Instead of insinuating wrongness when our values (or needs) haven't been met, NVC aims at communicating compassionately by identifying how we feel, what unmet need we have, and making a request of the other to help satisfy our need.

If we apply NVC to the above example, instead of saying "Violence is bad," we could say, "I'm fearful of the use of violence to resolve conflicts." Instead of the moralistic judgment, "people who kill others are evil," we could say instead, "I value resolving human conflict by other means." This informs people how you feel, what you value regarding resolving human conflict, and opens the possibility of choice.

According to Rosenburg's book, the NVC process involves four steps:

1. Observe what actions affect our well-being.

2. Notice how we feel in relation to what we observe.

3. Identify the needs, values, desires, etc. creating our feelings.

4. Identify concrete actions we can request to satisfy unmet needs and enrich our lives more.

LEARNING TO FEEL, NOT THINK

In his book, Rosenburg highlights the importance of distinguishing between real expression of emotions and statements which are descriptions of what we are thinking, not feeling. Often, people think they're expressing a feeling when, in fact, they're expressing an opinion, criticism, or a moral judgment. Here are some examples:

- When "I feel" is followed by "that" or "like" or "as if"; e.g., "I feel like you should know better."

- When "I feel" is used together with pronouns; e.g., "I feel I am constantly working."

- When "I feel" is used with names or nouns; e.g., "I feel Amy has acted irresponsibly."

None of these statements let the other person know what you are feeling. Despite prefacing with "I feel," each of the above three statements are expressions of what one thinks, not what one feels. Rosenburg's advice is that we should simply "name the emotion you are feeling without any judgment."

That's easy for him to say, is what I thought as I read his book. But I know firsthand putting a word or label to a feeling is not easy. Admittedly, Rosenburg never said it was; he just makes a valid point that until you let the other know how you are feeling, they are not likely to know, or they will assume they know.

I could relate to this point about mixing one's thoughts with what one is feeling, as I remember what my psychologist, Elizabeth, told me during one of our therapy sessions when I was diagnosed with clinical depression. I still remember the day, probably about the fourth or fifth session, when she asked me what I felt. I answered as best I could.

"Doris, every time I ask you how you feel, you tell me what you think," she said.

I just looked at her, not really understanding. "Yes, and so what?" I asked.

She replied, "I want to know what you feel, not what you're thinking about how you feel."

Elizabeth explained the difference between a feeling (an emotional response triggered by a bodily sensation) compared to a thought (cognitively processed interpretation or rationalization of an emotion).

"Oh, I see," I said, finally recognizing the difference. Then I confessed, "I don't know what I'm feeling."

This was the start of my road to recovery. Elizabeth asked me to start noticing more what I was feeling inside my body, the sensations, and what was going on inside of me. She asked me to try to express more of what I was feeling, instead of saying what I thought.

That was a lightbulb moment for me. I'd always known I had a preference for thinking over feeling when it comes to making decisions, ever since I took the Myers-Briggs Type Indicator psychometric test (see chapter two) and it revealed I was an ENTP type, with the T standing for "thinking." I'd been overusing this thinking preference to the detriment of my mental health.

Interesting how a little bit of knowledge or awareness can change so much. That evening, when I noticed the dirty dishes still left in the sink despite asking my husband on numerous occasions to put them in the dishwasher, instead of my normal response of just doing the dishes myself, I decided to "express my emotions more" and let rip with a torrent of anger and frustration. My husband had no idea what hit him and I felt so much better; though, of course, back then I didn't know about nonviolent communication, and thus hadn't yet learned how to communicate more compassionately.

WORDS TO EXPRESS EMOTIONS

Naming the emotion (how you are feeling) is a core element of nonviolent communication. A useful resource to help do that is contained in Professor Marc Brackett's book, *Permission to Feel: Unlock the Power of Emotions to Help Yourself and Your Child Thrive.* He's the founding director of the Yale Center for Emotional Intelligence, and developed a methodology called RULER as a way of expressing what's going on with you and communicating this to another.

RULER is an acronym for the following steps (Brackett 2019):

R = Recognizing: becoming aware of feelings

U = Understanding: how you process your feelings

L = Labeling: how you code or name what you feel

E = Expressing: you have a word or label for your feeling; you can say it and express it

R = Regulating emotion: a way of moderating the feeling through acknowledgment, time to process, label, and express it

The first important step is to notice you are experiencing a sensation somewhere inside your body. Some part is being triggered or stimulated; that's what Brackett means by Recognize. It starts in the body as an energetic vibration.

Next, categorize it as a "good or bad" or "positive or negative" feeling. That's about Understanding.

Here's the more difficult bit: Labeling. What do you call this feeling? The word we choose depends on our experiences and vocabulary. Brackett devised a useful two-dimensional way of mapping an emotion or feeling based on:

1. The level of energy felt, and

2. The level of pleasantness or unpleasantness.

MAPPING YOUR EMOTIONS

```
                        ┌─────────────┐
                        │ HIGH ENERGY │
                        └─────────────┘
                               ↑                    Estatic
        Enraged    Shocked     ¦
                               ¦        Cheerful
                Angry          ¦
      Anxious                  ¦    Pleasant
                    Annoyed    ¦                Blissful
┌──────────────┐               ¦                      ┌───────────────┐
│     LOW      │ ←─────────────┼──────────────────→   │     HIGH      │
│ PLEASANTNESS │               ¦                      │ PLEASANTNESS  │
└──────────────┘               ¦                      └───────────────┘
        Disgusted   Bored      ¦   Calm
                               ¦           Balanced
        Depressed              ¦       Relaxed
                    Drained    ¦   Relaxed      Serene
      Hopeless                 ↓
                        ┌─────────────┐
                        │ LOW ENERGY  │
                        └─────────────┘
```

I've populated each of the four quadrants with emotion words that feel right to me, but you might have other words to describe feelings in similar positions in each quadrant. That's okay. What's useful is to start building your emotions vocabulary by identifying words to express how you interpret the sensations you're experiencing. The more you can let others know how you are feeling, the fewer misunderstandings will occur.

For example, if you're experiencing high energy and low pleasantness, the top left quadrant, maybe you feel enraged, shocked, anxious, annoyed, or angry. I think the label I'd use to describe my feeling when I had my little tirade with my husband over the dishes was "angry."

If you're experiencing low energy and high pleasantness, the bottom right quadrant, maybe you feel calm, balanced, relaxed, restful, chilled, or serene.

If you are feeling a satisfactory level of pleasantness, regardless of how high or low energy, it's likely your needs are being met. However, if you're experiencing unpleasantness, regardless of energy levels, that's a sign you've got some unmet need. If that's the case, take some time out to reflect and ask yourself, "What's the unmet need, value, or desire behind this feeling I'm experiencing?"

The table on the next page identifies some basic needs we all have. Use this to help you pinpoint your unmet need when you experience unpleasant feelings when interacting with another person.

Some Basic Needs We All Have

Autonomy - To choose one's dreams, goals, values - To choose one's plan for fulfilling one's dreams, goals, values	**Integrity** - Authenticity - Creativity - Meaning - Self-worth
Celebration - To celebrate the creation of life and dreams fulfilled - To celebrate losses: loved ones, dreams, etc. (mourning)	**Play** - Fun - Laughter
Interdependence - Acceptance - Appreciation - Closeness - Community - Consideration - Contribution to the enrichment of life - Emotional safety - Empathy - Honest - Love - Reassurance - Respect - Support - Trust - Understanding - Warmth	**Spiritual Communion** - Beauty - Harmony - Inspiration - Order - Peace **Physical Nurturance** - Air - Food - Movement, exercise - Protection from life-threatening forms of life: viruses, bacteria, predatory animals - Rest - Sexual expression - Shelter - Touch - Water

KEY MESSAGES

- Becoming more compassionate to yourself and others is key to cultivating trust.

- Focus on your own feelings and needs instead of on what is wrong with others.

- When you are in touch with your own feelings and needs, you are able to ask for what you would like to have happen.

- Words and tone of voice can wound - be more intentional about how you express yourself and what kind of relationship you want to have with someone.

- When you communicate more from your heart, with compassion, others are more likely to understand your feelings and needs more.

- Your turn: improve and enhance your emotional vocabulary.

  - Create your own list of words for different emotions or feelings. Then draw your own "Mapping Your Emotions" grid and place each word on the map. Try to find words for each quadrant, depending on how energetic and how pleasant each emotion label feels.

  - For emotions that fall in the two "unpleasantness" quadrants, reflect on times you felt like that. What was happening? Where were you? Who else was with you?

  - Try and identify what unmet need, value, or desire could potentially be behind that feeling.

- Experiment with the NVC process to find a more compassionate way of expressing your feeling, what you value, and what you would like to have happen (i.e., make a request).

CHAPTER 10

THE SUCCESS OF FAILING

"Successful people don't spend their whole day succeeding."

I've had my share of bad things happen; disappointments, setbacks, and failures. These bad things have also had payoffs, contributing to building my resilience and shaping the path I'm on now. It's not just your abilities and talent bringing you success. What's even more important is your mindset—the set of beliefs affecting how you think, feel, and behave. All of this leads to cultivating trust in yourself, and trust in others; especially those in your social network.

This chapter is about developing a growth mindset, building resilience, and learning from failing and from adversity.

A GROWTH MINDSET

Carol Dweck, psychologist, professor at Stanford University, and author of *Mindset: The New Psychology of Success*, identified two types of mindsets in her book:

1. Fixed mindset: you believe your ability is set in stone and personality characteristics, talents, and abilities are finite or fixed and can't be changed or improved.

2. Growth mindset: the belief that your ability can change and grow. You believe intelligence and capability can be cultivated.

I'm deliberately choosing to develop a deeper growth mindset for myself, as well as encouraging my coaching clients to do the same, because I see the benefit and value in doing so. A growth mindset views failures and mistakes not as limits, but rather as tools that inform you, liberate you, and allow you to find value, joy, and success in the process, regardless of the outcome.

Most of our core beliefs are formed when we were children, unconsciously absorbing information or opinions from our parents, family, environment, school, and friends. When we're young, we're not able to discern between what's true and what's false. Beliefs can be empowering or limiting. Limiting beliefs hold us back, give rise to negative thoughts and emotions, and prevent us from achieving our potential. On the other hand, empowering or positive beliefs allow us to believe in ourselves, take action to get what we want, and develop resilience. Remember, a belief is only a "thought" you think, or perceive, to be true.

REFRAMING

Cultivating a growth mindset begins with shifting your inner dialogue from limiting beliefs about your ability to beliefs about your opportunities and needs. If there is something you want but believe or think it's not possible to have, then that's a sign you may have a limiting belief. You can shift that belief by reframing or restating it.

For example, instead of thinking, "I'm terrible at public speaking and giving presentations," reframe that thought to something like, "I need more practice at speaking and presenting in front of others," or "I want to get better at public speaking." Similarly, instead of thinking "I'm not good enough to be promoted," that thought could become, "I need some additional experience before I'll be ready for promotion."

Simple restatements have a dramatic impact on what you believe about your own abilities. Turning these negative beliefs into affirmations can help encourage and motivate us, especially when you repeat them to yourself daily. This is something I do as part of my regular yoga practice.

Stating affirmations in terms of learning goals is a great way to begin to change your thinking patterns about yourself.

- "I can learn and develop."

- "I can manage my own time."

- "I can commit to practicing to get better."

LEARNING FROM FAILURE

Having a growth mindset is choosing to believe in the positive attitude behind failure. Namely, to see failing as part of learning. When you choose to try to do something, that's a decision. It takes effort to try, especially something not easily within your reach or where you lack experience or skill. It can also take determination, persistence, practice, and a willingness to learn from all your efforts. And, as founder of the entrepreneurial YO! Sushi restaurant chain, Simon Woodroffe, knows, it also requires a willingness to fail:

"The only thing that I have ever found that is common to just about all successful people is that successful people don't spend their whole day succeeding...The people that are most successful are the ones that are willing to fail."

Some of the most successful people in this world got to where they are because they failed, not just once or twice or three times, but sometimes hundreds and thousands. Take, for example, Michael Jordan, the famous basketball player. He has said, "I've missed more than nine thousand shots in my career. I've lost almost 300 games. Twenty-six times, I've been trusted to take the game winning shot and missed. I've failed over and over and over again in my life. And that is why I succeed."

Or James Dyson, the inventor of the bagless vacuum cleaner. Do you know how many prototypes he made before he got it right? Ten? Fifty? One hundred? Actually, it was 5,126. He had 5,126 failures, but he learned from each one and after fifteen years, he finally invented his first successful model: the Dyson we know today. As Dyson said, "It didn't happen overnight, but after years of testing, tweaking, fist-banging, and after more than five thousand prototypes, it was there. Or nearly there. I still needed to manufacture it and go sell it" (Malone-Kircher, 2016).

BUILDING RESILIENCE

One of the lessons in learning to trust yourself is about learning who you are and what you are capable of. When bad things happen, we don't just get over it, we learn from it, adapt, and develop. People refer to this as resilience: "the capacity to recover quickly from difficulties" (Lexico).

To build resilience, you need to want to learn and be willing to put in the effort and time required. That's about becoming an "intentional learner," someone who embraces the need to learn from everyday experiences and interactions. Having a growth mindset is one of two critical factors that helps to orientate you toward learning in everything you do. The other factor is curiosity and being aware and open to ideas and making connections between disparate things (Christensen 2020).

Consider strengthening your curiosity muscle, which in turn builds resilience, by adopting practices like:

- Facing your fears. Take some time to reflect on what you are afraid of. Maybe it's asking questions in meetings, speaking in public, or asking for help. Once you can identify what you are fearful of, you can decide on—or at least, take a first step toward—how to address it. This demonstrates stages two and three of the Conscious Competence model outlined in chapter eight.

- Focus on what you love doing, do it more often, and do it in different contexts. This is about using and developing your strengths, which we looked at in chapter five.

- Find new and novel experiences to try. This could be going to visit a museum, gallery, theater, library, sports or music performance, or learning a new language or instrument. Or reading a book or watching a documentary you know nothing about. Just go somewhere or do something you've never tried before. Experiment and see what happens. These are all examples of exploring the "Unknown" quadrant in the Johari Window, which we looked at in chapter two.

FROM RESILIENCE TO ANTI-FRAGILITY

Anti-fragility goes beyond robustness or resilience and means something or someone does not merely withstand a shock but actually improves because of it (Taleb, 2012).

Anti-fragility, a concept developed by Professor Nassim Nicholas Taleb, is about learning to make our public and private lives stronger from embracing shocks and uncertainty more, rather than simply being less vulnerable to randomness and chaos. He divides people into three categories:

- Fragile: when you avoid disorder and disruption because you fear the mess you might make of your life. You might believe you're keeping safe, but this could also make yourself even more vulnerable, as any disorder and disruption or shock could tear everything apart much more easily if it happens.

- Robust (or resilient): when you can stand up to shocks and recover, without flinching and without changing who you are.

- Anti-fragile: when shocks and disruptions make you stronger and more creative, and better able to adapt to each new challenge you face, thus developing and growing your capacity to embrace and learn from change.

I appreciate the benefits of becoming more anti-fragile, especially in this increasingly uncertain, volatile, complex, and ambiguous (VUCA) world. Learning to embrace disruptions and shocks—events one doesn't have any control over—is like learning to ride the waves while maintaining balance in your life. To do that well takes daily practice—something we'll look at in more detail in the next chapter.

My experience of bad things happening to me have not only helped build my resilience, they have also been instrumental in my development, making me more anti-fragile. Experiences like when I suffered clinical depression or was told to resign from a job at which I thought I performed reasonably well have helped me to build my confidence, efficacy, and self-assurance that I can deal with whatever comes my way.

Other people have told me how bad things in their life have helped them become more resilient and anti-fragile. Take my writing colleague, Nils, who told me about his experience getting conned when he was nineteen years old traveling solo around Europe on his gap year before starting university. He got duped by a very clever con man, who persuaded him that he personally would get a much better local currency exchange rate for Nils' US dollars. The con man won his trust and Nils handed over all his nine hundred dollars. That was the last Nils was to see of his money and the con man, and the experience shook Nils' confidence and trust in himself.

"I felt like the ground had given way beneath my feet. And especially because there had been warning signs, and there were obstacles in my way. Yet I persisted in overcoming those obstacles, just to lose all my money!" he told me. He felt tremendous anger and guilt and decided to punish himself by surviving on just bread and water and sleeping under the skies.

However, Nils discovered during his first couple of nights of doing this, that the people he met along the way were extremely generous, helpful, and kind. They invited him to eat with them and stay in their homes. His trust in humanity was restored, which helped him to regain some trust in himself.

"At some point, I realized I'm young, and I'm traveling around Europe," he recounted, before saying as much to me as to himself, "You have permission to enjoy life again."

Being able to reflect on his situation and what he learned about himself helped Nils to forgive himself and move on. I asked him how he compares his trust in himself now, some thirty years on. He said, "I know my weaknesses now much better than I did in the past. I don't know if I can say trust in myself is higher or lower. But in the past, it was based on maybe ideas about myself that weren't necessarily accurate. Now, it's more grounded in reality. It's based on a more accurate sense of self."

Nils went on to tell me about the twist in his tale of adversity in his youth. When he applied to graduate school a few years later, he was asked to submit an essay about a time when he was severely challenged. "I recounted my story about being conned, and on the strength of that story, I ended up getting a $10,000 scholarship. And that scholarship was repeated in the second year."

Nils' story demonstrates how, with time, you not only learn more about yourself, but you can build strength from adversity. It also illustrates how one event at one time can lead to unknown consequences at another time (an example also of the non-linear nature of Emergent Knowledge as discussed in chapter six).

When bad things happen to you, how accurate is your sense of self? What are you basing your assessment on? What needs to happen for you to reflect, learn, and move on?

COOPERATION AND SOCIAL NETWORKS

One important lesson in building resilience is to ask for help when you need or want it. So often people don't ask for help because they think it's a sign of weakness, they don't know what help they would like, or they don't know who to ask. Surveys of successful businesspeople reveal asking for help is a skill they wish they had developed when they looked back at their younger self as they climbed the corporate ladder (Poole, 2017).

When I became a parent, I struggled at first to juggle childcare with my work commitments. After I got over my initial embarrassment of asking for help, I found I could call on other mothers, and sometimes fathers, for favors such as school pick-ups and drop-offs, arranging playdates, and more. It turned out other parents needed help sometimes too, and this mutual reciprocity helped build and expand my social network.

At the basis of all relationships is cooperation, and humans are the most cooperative species on the planet. The result of this need to cooperate with each other is that we build a network of relationships, beginning with support from friends, family, and the people you love (Machin, 2021).

I found it fascinating to learn research has shown such a network of relationships is organized into distinct layers with a finite number in each layer. Within this network, members interact in broadly similar ways regardless of age, personality, gender, ethnic background, or other individual differences. The limit of an active network of relationships is 150. This is known as Dunbar's number, named after Oxford professor Robin Dunbar. His research looked at social interactions from groups all around the world as diverse as European mobile-phone users, to African hunter-gather tribes, to factory employees (Dunbar, 1992).

Because social skills are important in juggling the complex world of social relationships, a person's ability to understand another person's perspective varies and is also limited by one's cognitive processing capabilities. There's only so much information you can remember and keep in your head.

The layers Dunbar defined go like this:

- Loved ones: the tightest circle has just five people we are emotionally closest to and with whom we interact most often, at least weekly. These may be your parents, partner, children, or best friends. These are the people you turn to at your most emotionally difficult times, and you know they will respond and support you.

- Good friends: in total about fifteen and includes your loved ones. This group includes people who you enjoy socializing with, such as going out for the night, to the bar, movies, or restaurant.

- Friends: a total of fifty, which include extended family, acquaintances, and some work colleagues.

- Meaningful contacts: a total of 150. You know each person in this group and can recall your relationship with them, although contact may be infrequent.

Representation of Dunbar's Number

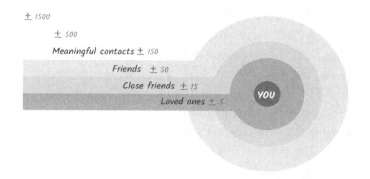

Beyond the 150, there could be another 350 acquaintances you may have met or know in passing, making a total of five hundred relationships in your network. After that layer, there might be a further thousand people who you can recognize but have no relationship with, such as celebrities, politicians, and people in the news. (Dunbar 1992)

Of course, these numbers represent a range. Extroverts tend to have a larger network and spread themselves more thinly across their friends, while introverts concentrate on a smaller pool of "thick" contacts. Women also tend to have slightly more contacts within the closest layers (Dunbar 1992).

COMMUNITIES OF SUPPORT

When I first read about Dunbar's research, I thought about my own social network in terms of the layers of different relationship structures. While the actual numbers differ, they are roughly in that order of magnitude. My loved ones are people I've known for several decades, and while I have several hundred acquaintances thanks to social media like LinkedIn, Facebook, and Instagram, I don't really know them.

In terms of the 150 I do know, I know them reasonably well—at least, well enough to ask for help if I needed to. When I looked closely at my 150, I could identify clusters of relationships which I call my "communities of support" for different aspects of my life. For example, in writing this book, I've been part of a large community of aspiring authors and within that community, I've formed closer relationships with about five people. In fact, one of them is Nils! We've connected with other authors whose books have similar themes to ours, and provide mutual support, feedback, and ideas for marketing efforts.

Additionally, as I've mentioned before, I'm also part of the Toastmasters International public speaking community. While there are over 350,000 members, my own closer contacts would number about twenty.

Take time to look at your own social network. Identify the people who can help you develop your strengths and passions, and be there for support in times of adversity, thus building your own resilience and becoming more anti-fragile over time.

KEY MESSAGES

- Attitudes, like mindsets, are not set in stone. You can choose to develop a deeper growth mindset and become more curious to continually learn and develop yourself.

- Take a more positive perspective, especially when bad things happen. Become more aware of how you talk to yourself when things go wrong. Take time to reflect and learn from the experience.

- To get what you want takes time, practice, perseverance, and determination. Treat failing as a positive sign that you are trying. Learning to trust yourself more is about allowing yourself to try, and try again, for what you want.

- Use your social network to support you when you fail and help you build resilience, particularly the fifteen or so good friends, including loved ones. Remember, relationships are about cooperation, mutual reciprocity, and compassion, as discussed in chapter nine.

- Your turn. Take some time to reflect on your attitude and mindset and how this has helped or hindered you in developing relationships.

    – What kind of mindset would you like to have and why?

    – What kind of beliefs do you have about yourself that help and hinder you?

    – Who are your loved ones and good friends whom you can rely on when you need to?

CHAPTER 11

CULTIVATING HEALTHY HABITS

"To be is better than to seem to be."

When I was in my teens and attending Taieri High School in New Zealand, the school's motto was "Esse Quam Videri," meaning "to be is better than to seem to be." That made intuitive sense; be real and true to who you are. But of course, when you're young, you don't really know who you are. In many ways, that's what life's about—go out into the world and explore. Get an education and experience and discover who you really want to become.

The school's motto shines a light on the essence of living a good and meaningful life. That's about developing habits supporting your physical and emotional well-being and aligned to your values. Habits are just things you do often and regularly, sometimes without knowing you're doing them (similar to the level of skill as in "unconscious competence" as discussed in chapter eight). There's good habits, like daily brushing our teeth and making our bed, and not so good ones, like drinking too much alcohol or eating too much.

When we cultivate healthy habits, it makes it easier to withstand adversity or hardships that might come our way.

You can become calmer and more grounded, in your everyday life, enabling and empowering you to decide the direction you want to go in life and what you'd like to have happen with a clearer mind. In turn, you'll develop more trust in yourself, thus it becomes a self-reinforcing positive cycle.

It's taken me most of my life to develop healthy habits and to find my path. Paradoxically, it's about coming home to ourselves. The answers are inside each of us when we allow ourselves the time and space to explore, experience, evolve, and emerge more fully. This, I believe, is the essence of Buddhist monk and peace activist Thích Nhất Hạnh's quote: "the way out is in."

In this chapter, I'll share how I've come to develop some of my daily healthy habits like meditation and yoga, and what I'm learning from these practices. But first, I'd like to introduce you to a wider framework called *ikigai* (pronounced ee-key-guy) as I believe it provides a useful perspective for viewing the reasons behind cultivating healthy habits and how it builds trust in yourself.

IKIGAI

In Japanese, IKI (生き) means "alive" or "life." GAI (甲斐) means "benefit" or "worth." Thus IKIGAI means, "that which gives your life worth, meaning, or purpose." It's about the art of living a meaningful life (Garcia and Miralles, 2016).

With greater self-awareness of how you came to be where you are physically, emotionally, and mentally, and greater understanding and appreciation of your personal values and strengths, you're more enabled and empowered to design and create the life you want.

I first came across the concept of *ikigai* when I read Hector Garcia and Francesc Miralles' book, *Ikigai: The Japanese Secret to a Long and Happy Life.* They studied why there are so many centenarians living on the Japanese island of Okinawa. For every 100,000 inhabitants, there are 24.5 people over the age of 100, which is far more than the global average. Not only do Okinawan people live much longer than the rest of the world's population, they also have far fewer cases of chronic illnesses such as cancer and heart disease, and the rate of dementia is well below the global average (Garcia and Miralles, 2016).

As the diagram below shows, *ikigai* is the intersection of four spheres: passion, profession, vocation, and mission. It can take time and experience to discover your own responses to each sphere. You must have lived and tried different things, and you must notice what's working for you and what's not.

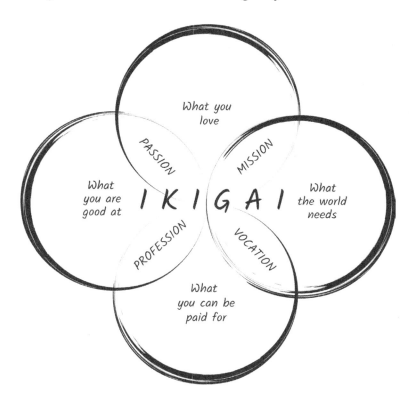

I'm confident I've found my *ikigai*. I love my vocation as a coach because I am satisfying my passion for curiosity. I'm doing what I love and using my strengths like listening, asking questions, analyzing patterns, and making connections. I also get paid (most of the time). As a group facilitator, I help others to develop their fuller potential. They become more enlightened, happier, and empowered individuals who go on to inspire and motivate others. Helping to develop people happy in themselves and living in harmony with nature and the wider community—that is my mission.

Hopefully, if you've been reflecting on the questions and exercises posed at the end of each chapter in this book, you'll be able to use the *ikigai* model to assess where you are. What's your passion, profession, vocation, and mission? What are you doing at the intersection of each sphere?

A WESTERN PERSPECTIVE

Another way of looking at *ikigai* from a more Western perspective and the realities of modern urban life is to consider Charles Duhigg's definition of productivity. Duhigg is an American journalist and author of S*marter Faster Better: The Secrets of Being Productive in Life and Business.* He defines productivity as "getting things done without sacrificing everything we care about along the way."

This is firstly about identifying what actually matters most to you: your values. It's also about identifying your goals or desired outcomes. What would you like to have happen?

The point behind Duhigg's definition of productivity is recognizing you have to make choices. Review your priorities from time to time to see if your to do list is still relevant or not. You may need to adapt and rearrange priorities in light of your circumstances.

You have to pay attention to yourself and allocate time to take care of your physical and emotional well-being and health so you can live well and support others you care about.

BALANCING WORK, REST, AND PLAY

In chapter four, we looked at the impact of physiology and neurology on our psyche and well-being and the importance of taking time to rest and digest to allow for recovery. In chapter seven, we looked at the construct of time, and the importance of establishing a rhythm of activities facilitating optimal performance (i.e., day-to-day living with joy and vitality) while, again, allowing for time to rest and digest. Chapter ten examined how to build resilience and anti-fragility by embracing a growth mindset and curiosity to inevitable challenges and disruptions.

Given all we know now, I want to focus on some practical things we can do to help us cultivate habits to help sustain and strengthen us each and every day.

Cultivating healthy habits is about balancing your day between work, rest, and play. Depending on your situation, work could consist of paid or unpaid employment; basically, rewarding activities you engage in, whether in monetary or non-monetary terms (satisfaction, pride, community spirit). Whether you're a mother, caregiver, teacher, employee, manager, or boss, you've got work to do. It's important to have breaks during the day, not just to consume food and liquids for nutritional reasons, but also for the mind to pause too. Even when you are in a flow state—focused and concentrating on a task at hand—you will not sustain that flow for too long; the brain just isn't wired that way. Taking time to pause can open new pathways and gain space in your mind.

Looking at rest, which, together with time to pause during the day, typically means sleep. The younger you are, the more sleep you will need. Children between six and thirteen should sleep for nine to eleven hours a night, while teenagers need about eight to ten hours to function at their best. For adults, it's about seven or eight hours a night, but that can vary considerably (Suni, 2021).

Play consists of recreation, like sports or exercise, dancing or singing, playing cards or video games, meeting up with friends, going out on a date, or having a party; all these activities are forms of play. The amount of time you allocate for play is a personal one, as is when to play. If you've got a full-time job, that might mean devoting more of your weekends to playing. The important point is you allow yourself to play, not just for pure enjoyment, but to realize it's a key ingredient for living well and connecting with others. There's also a neurological benefit with play: it activates more of the right hemisphere of your brain, which is more about creativity and possibilities.

For myself, I've found that nowadays I only need about six hours of sleep at night, and I often wake up before dawn. I enjoy the peace and quiet with time for myself, a bit of exercise to stretch my body, and reading and writing in my diary. I also look at the weather forecast and plan what I will do. Morning time is my time to play, as well as have a bit of conscious reflection time without any disturbances.

I wasn't always like this. When my daughters were little, my mornings were busy getting them ready for school: getting them up and dressed, making packed lunches, cooking breakfast (which often ended up being eaten in the car), and the housework, as well as fitting in my paid work.

When I was younger, I found it a struggle to get out of bed, even without being clinically depressed. I used to marvel at how both my parents got up at about five in the morning most days. My mother cleaned, fed the chickens, and prepared food for the day. My father was up even earlier at least twice a week when he'd drive the lorry loaded with produce to be auctioned at the wholesale vegetable market in the city.

I realize now that early mornings were their time to work, while for me, being a child, it was my time to rest. It was in the evenings I saw my parents relax and play a little, with my father reading his Chinese newspaper and my mother watching TV or writing letters to her siblings. Thus, this goes to show that at different times and ages in our lives, we have different responsibilities and will require different schedules and percentages for balancing, work, rest, and play.

MEDITATION AND YOGA

Meditation is a practice that has helped me gain space in my mind; the kind of space Viktor Frankl refers to where "the power to choose our response" lies and the space leading to our growth and freedom (see chapter four). Meditation is a catch-all word for a myriad of varieties of contemplative practice (Goleman 2017).

Different people will resonate with different practices. My interpretation of a meditation practice is an opportunity to just be and allow your brain waves to quiet and settle. I've tried a few different approaches over the years until I found one that feels right for me. When you find a meditative practice that resonates with you, it's much easier to maintain it. My encouragement to you is to keep searching and experimenting until you find a form that feels right for you.

Yoga is a form of moving meditation to build resilience in the mind and body. I have been practicing yoga on and off over the years, just doing it once a week at most. But during the first lockdown due to the COVID-19 pandemic in March 2020, I discovered free yoga on YouTube, as did many millions around the world. It's a practice I've come to love and continue to do daily in the morning just after my meditation practice.

I do both my meditation and yoga practices first thing in the morning—my dedicated and precious time totally just for me. To be by myself, with myself, alone. I enjoy it and it's a habit I easily maintain because:

1. It allows me to slow down.

2. It enables me to spend time with myself, with nowhere to go, and nothing to do.

3. I feel calm and at peace, and it sets me up for my day.

Since 2015, I've listened to meditations by William Yensen, an integrative therapist working with the body, mind, and spirit. I was recommended his meditations on YouTube by friends experienced in *tai chi*, a Chinese martial art embracing the mind, body, and spirit. There's something about Yensen's voice, words, and the silence between the words I really like. I sit, eyes closed, noticing my breath as it moves in and out of my body and follow his guidance.

After years of listening to his meditations, I was curious to find out how he came to do what he does and arranged to interview him for this book. A Canadian by birth, and now living in Germany, Yensen described himself as "a researcher and explorer of life." He's also a certified yoga, meditation, and mindfulness teacher and energy healer with over seventeen years of counseling experience.

"For me, this work is simply a natural impulse within myself," he said. "It's a passion to explore and expand and to engage with others who are interested in that exploration and want to experience healing and discover the miraculous within themselves."

I'm someone interested in exploring and discovering "the miraculous within themselves," and so I wanted to know more from this teacher, as it's clear to me he's found his *ikigai*.

That "natural impulse" goes back to when he was a young boy growing up in the countryside in Canada. He told me he was often left to tend the fire as wood burned, so he'd find himself staring at the flames for hours on end. Though he had no idea what meditation was at the time, he recalled how those solitary experiences of watching the flames felt as if he was one with the fire.

OPENING TO THE UNKNOWN

One of his meditations, called Opening to the Unknown, is about "arriving in this present moment with a beginner's mind, fresh to experience yourself, just as you are now, making space for new experience." For me, that describes precisely the state I want to inhabit more of the time and not just when I'm meditating.

Yensen went on to explain how we can become more effective when we practice "transitioning more smoothly" between activities in daily life. Often people look at what they do in a day as "discrete activities": meditating, eating breakfast, working, spending time with the kids, watching TV, etc. But there is a space between each discrete activity; time coming into and moving from each activity. It's about becoming more conscious and mindful to the present moment, while maintaining a sense of that feeling of being grounded, centered, and calm you get when in meditation.

One reason why I love Yensen's meditations so much is because they are "somatic" meditations focused on getting you connected with your body and listening and learning from the wisdom within. By paying exquisite attention to sensations you experience, without judgment and without your mind trying to interpret meaning, there's the possibility you will uncover what is *already* there. His somatic meditations help to develop capacity and ability to, as he phrases it, "bring your state of meditation with you into your day, into your evening, and into your life." That state of meditation is one where you are "letting go of old strategies, thoughts or feelings about how to meditate. Let your body be your guide. Let your breath be your guide."

I'd like to quote a passage from his "Opening to the Unknown" meditation as it sums up the experience so well:

"Every moment, life is changing.

Sometimes more subtly and sometimes more dramatically.

When we open to this phenomenon of change,

when we recognize the truth of change,

and allow ourselves to ground in the present moment,

and be open to the possibilities of creativity now,

how might it be if I relax and open?

What might I become if I let this change happen?"

In so many ways, his words echo the meaning behind Lao Tzu's aphorism which I quoted in my Introduction:

"When you let go of what you are, you become what you might be."

RULES FOR LIVING

After I reviewed Garcia and Miralles' research and key findings about *ikigai*, I combined them with the lessons I've learned in my life. I developed these nine healthy habits, or rules, to build trust and live a meaningful life:

• Stay active, mentally and physically: don't just "retire" from paid employment, but consider using your skills, strengths, and experience in other contexts, such as volunteering, setting up your own venture or business, or mentoring younger people. Don't give up on doing the things you love and do well just because you're not getting paid anymore.

• Slow down and stay curious: take time to pause and reflect more often; be open to learning.

• Move everyday: walk, run, cycle, play a sport, dance - it's important to stretch and keep the body moving.

• Eat nutritious food, but not too much: eat to be 80 percent full, as less is more when it comes to eating for long life.

• Connect with nature and the natural world: go outdoors at least once a day and breathe in some fresh air. Remember the effect of nature on stressed patients in the Alnarp Rehabilitation Garden from chapter seven.

- Surround yourself with good friends: identify your 150 (see Dunbar's number in chapter ten), particularly your top five loved ones, your fifteen good friends, and the fifty friends in your social network.

- Smile more: not only does it exercise your facial muscles, smiling releases endorphins and serotonin, thus reducing stress and pain, making you more attractive, helping you stay positive, and lengthening your life.

- Give thanks: to your ancestors, to nature, the food you eat, to friends and family, to everyone and everything that brightens your day.

- Live in the moment: stop regretting the past and fearing the future. Today is all there is. Make the most of it.

KEY MESSAGES

There are only twenty-four hours in a day, and how you use those hours affects the quality of your life. It's important to balance your time between work, rest, and play; all three types of activities are vital and contribute to your well-being. Then you trust yourself more and trust yourself first, enabling you to cultivate healthy relationships with those you love.

Take time to reflect on where you are now, physically, mentally, and emotionally. Consider the following:

- Recognize the changes in your life, possibly due to the pandemic and subsequent lockdowns and restrictions. How have you responded or reacted to these changes?

- What kind of balance do you have in terms of work, rest, and play?

  - What would you like to have more or less of?

  - And what needs to happen for that change in balance to happen?

- What habits do you have contributing to a healthy and desired way of living?

  - What habits do you have that hinder this way of living that you would like to change?

  - Then, thinking about what you'd like to change, ask yourself, "What would I like to have happen?"

- Do you have a meditation or mindfulness practice? If not, consider exploring and trying a meditative practice - remember, it takes time for a habit to form; be gentle and compassionate with yourself and try not to judge yourself.

  - You can start right now with this small step: consciously focus your attention on your breath as you breathe in. Hold for a second, then breathe out. Hold for a second and repeat.

    - You can do this any way you like: sitting on the floor or a chair or standing; eyes open or closed. Set a timer for one minute. You can progressively increase the time as you like.

EPILOGUE

"Nourish your original breath."

As mentioned in the Introduction, I structured the book in three parts, each corresponding to my ACB model of growth and change: Awareness, Choices, Behave. I also used a symbol for each part of the book: the *Anja* for Awareness, the *Koru* for Choices, and the *Yin-Yang* for Behave (and Balance) because, as the age-old adage in multiple languages say, "a picture is worth a thousand words."

You may have noticed the image I used to depict my 4C model of trust is similar to the *Anja* symbol. That's an example of synchronicity at work, similar to six iterations of an Emergent Knowledge process (see chapter six) as I was working with my publisher's design team to create the image.

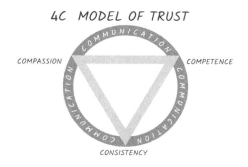

My hope is you are now more aware, more informed, and more knowledgeable about what makes you tick, and more willing and able to trust yourself and others. Awareness or knowing is one thing and taking action or doing is something else. I hope you are also motivated and inspired to become more of the person you were born, and want, to be.

A final Clean question I'd like to pose: for you, trust is like what?

For me, trust is like an emerging heart, pulsating with the rhythm of life, and radiating the possibilities for joy, peace, and love.

Throughout this book, I've quoted from many sources: my teachers and tutors, friends, family, colleagues, clients, researchers, and other authors, as well as those creators who, though they have departed this Earth, leave behind their wonderful legacy of concepts, theories, processes, and practices.

I believe these creators, like Carl Rogers, David Grove, and Marshall Rosenburg, were imbued with a spirit of selfless generosity, not just because I've been told this by people who knew or worked closely with them, but it's a feeling I get when I read their writings or watch them on YouTube videos. Another key influence for me in writing this book is the Chinese philosopher and sage, Lao Tzu, and his words of wisdom captured in his aphorisms.

I started this book with a quotation from Lao Tzu: "When you let go of what you are, you become what you might be." I'd like to close with a story about him I read in the introduction of one of my favorite books on Clean Language: *Trust Me, I'm the Patient,* written by playwright, scriptwriter, and Clean Language and Emergent Knowledge psychotherapist, Philip Harland, who worked closely with David Grove for many years.

Master Lao Tzu asked Gatekeeper Yin:

"How can I walk underwater and not drown, move through fire without burning, and pass amongst the multitude of forms of life without fear?"

Gatekeeper Yin replied: "You must learn to move within limits which have no limit and to journey to where both the start and the end of all life is."

"How can I do this?" asked Lao Tzu.

Gatekeeper Yin replied: "You must nourish your original breath."

Lao Tzu's question to Gatekeeper Yin is universal: how does one live life well without fear? The answer he is given is as much of a riddle. How do you "nourish your original breath?" That's the question I've been exploring in this book.

When I asked Philip what led him to choose this story, he referred me back to what he wrote in his book: "I have two objectives... to present the case for achieving healing, change, and self-knowledge with minimal outside intervention; and to outline a number of new ways of doing that which are simple, practical, powerful, and proven."

That is why I love using Clean Language and Emergent Knowledge processes in my work as a coach and in everyday conversations with a light touch. Learning about the approach and philosophy of Clean has helped me to rediscover and nourish my original breath. It's led me to reflect, research, and remember where I came from, how I came to know what I know, and how I came to be where I am now. In doing so, I've learned—with the help and support of many people past and present—to trust myself more.

Over time and space, that breath changes. The search to find one's original breath is the quest to find your whole integrated self. That quest is a lifelong journey, from where both the start and the end of all life is. I'm not a philosopher, but for me, I can translate Gatekeeper Yin's answer to Lao Tzu's universal question into practical terms:

- Examine your life and identify when your breath changed— the critical times in your life when something happened that impacted and changed you and the path you took.

- Nourish that breath with healthy habits: good nutrition, time to do the things you love, sufficient and good quality sleep, work aligned to your strengths and values and serving others in this world.

- Connect with others and find communities to belong; listen, inquire with curiosity, share, give, and receive with a spirit of generosity.

When we choose to do these things more, and actually do them, we become more appreciative of our past, our ancestors, family and friends. We become more confident in our strengths and abilities, and less fearful of your weaknesses and the prospect of failure. We become more excited for our future and more open to the unknown. We become more honest, committed, and supportive of relationships with ourselves and others.

Trust in the process.

Trust in your healthy habits.

Trust yourself first.

RESOURCES

CLEAN LANGUAGE AND EMERGENT KNOWLEDGE
In chapter six, I introduced Clean Language and Emergent Knowledge, created by New Zealand psychotherapist David Grove. He seldom wrote anything down himself, but thanks to the dedicated work of James Lawley and Penny Tompkins, there is now a rich collection of information and resources about Grove's life work. Their website, https://www.cleanlanguage.co.uk/, is a rich repository for material concerning Grove's work.

Other useful websites for information and training in Clean Language and Emergent Knowledge include:

Clean Learning:
https://cleanlearning.co.uk/

The Clean Coaching Center:
https://cleancoaching.com/

Clean Language Institute:
https://cleanlanguagetraining.com/

Clean Language Resource Centre:
https://www.cleanlanguageresources.com/

BOOKS ABOUT CLEAN LANGUAGE
AND EMERGENT KNOWLEDGE

Clean Coaching: The Insider Guide to Making Change Happen by Angela Dunbar.

The Work and Life of David Grove: Clean Language and Emergent Knowledge by Carol Wilson.

From Curiosity to Contempt: Creating the Conditions for Groups to Collaborate by Caitlin Walker.

Clean Language: Revealing Metaphors and Opening Minds by Wendy Sullivan and Judy Rees.

Hope in the Corner of My Heart: A Healing Journey through the Dream-Logical World of Inner Metaphors by Gina Campbell.

Metaphors in the Mind: Transformation Through Symbolic Modelling by James Lawley and Penny Tompkins.

Trust Me, I'm the Patient: Clean Language, Metaphor, and the New Psychology of Change by Philip Harland.

Clean Approaches for Coaches: How to Create Conditions for Change Using Clean Language and Symbolic Modeling by Marian Way.

NONVIOLENT COMMUNICATIONS (NVC)

If you'd like to learn more about NVC, check out Marshall Rosenburg's website for more resources: www.nonviolentcommunication.com

You may also like to take a look at the Center for Nonviolent Communications for resources and training: www.cnvc.org/about

ACKNOWLEDGMENTS

Having an idea is one thing and putting it into action is quite something else. I had an idea and a dream to write a book; something about my life and what I've come to know about living. I'd made many starts in the past, but the writing never got very far. Then, about one year ago, my colleague, Navid Nazeman, mentioned he was in a book writing course with Georgetown University's Creator Institute. Thanks to Navid, I joined Professor Eric Koester's course and the rest is history.

Big thanks to Eric and his team for our weekly Zoom sessions, as I learned about the art of what makes a good story and encouraging me to try out different ways of writing. A specific shoutout to my developmental editor, Cass Lauer, who was at my side with encouraging and helpful feedback on an array of stories, and for getting me to my first draft manuscript stage.

To Brian Bies and the publishing team at New Degree Press for some amazing guidance on transforming that draft to this finished book. Thank you to my acquiring editor, Tasslyn Magnusson, for your insightful advice on my personal narrative, Jess Beach and Amanda Brown in copy editing, and particularly to my marketing and revisions editor, Caitlyn Conville, for keeping me on track and supporting me through the process. Thank you also to John Saunders for motivating me during my Indiegogo fundraising and pre-sales campaign, and to Gjorgji Pejkouski, Nikola Tikoski and the creative team for the book cover design and images.

In addition, I'd like to thank everyone I've interviewed during the course of researching and writing this book, in particular Julia Vaughn Smith, Caitlin Walker, Carol Wilson, William Yensen, Judy Rees, Nils Junge, Steve Craig, and Susie Kong. Special thanks also to Antony Young for his marketing insights and his creative team in Wellington, and to Matthew Hudson and his Emerging Knowledge process, "Experiment Number Four," which came just at the right time to help me recall significant stories for this book.

Thank you to my team of beta-readers whose feedback on draft chapters enabled me to craft the words to another level: Sarah Eze, Julia Feng, Sara Goodworth, Fiona Hoang, Lindsey Lunn, and Tiggy Munnelly.

And a huge thank you to everyone in my author community, a diverse group of people from thirteen countries, for giving me your support. This book is for you:

Ai Tin Ho	Arnold Young
Alex Goodworth	Axel Thill
Amanda Sew Hoy	Beth Hughes
Amy Corday	Beverley Wong Nam
Angela Dunbar	Bill Critchley
Angela Rigby	Bohwon Kim
Ann Marie Choie	Cameron Sew Hoy
Annabel Lunn	Carolyn Munday
Anne Downing	Cass Lauer
Anthony Chin	Chantel Curwen

Chris Marsh
Chris Sew Hoy
Chris Roberts
Christine Goodworth
Christine Roux
Christopher Fung
David Ross,
Deborah Hayden
Diana Choie
Dilys Tan
Eddy Quah
Esther Joe
Fanny Bourgeois
Fiona Au
Fiona Hoang
Fiona Johnstone
Frances Clemmow
Geoff Bascand
Geoffrey Lorigan
Gill Mogg-Smith
Gillian Prior
Gina Campbell
Grace Chung
Hani Law
Hannah Hoang
Haydn Dias
Helen Scott

Ian Scott
Irene Kuhn
Ivan Young
Jack Sew Hoy
Jackie Crombie
Jackie Lawlor
James Goodworth
Janice & Peter Sew Hoy
Jaqueline Ching
Jeni Butcher
Jennifer Yee Collinson
Jill Harris
Jon Donald
Julia Feng,
Justin Sew Hoy
Kam Trigg
Karen Davies
Kate Lee
Katherine Galliano
Katherine Goodman
Kevin Sew Hoy
King King Tsang
Lance Young,
Lin Keelaghan
Linder Chong
Lindsey Lunn
Lorraine Proud

Lutuf Shah

Marcus Croman

Marcus Sew Hoy

Marietta Gardner

Marian Way

Marion Von Groenheim

Marion Young

Mark Juson

Mark Peacock

Matthew Ngan

Matthew Gnagi

Michael Brent

Michelle Lucas

Mike B.

Morgan Chambers

Natalie Sew Hoy

Nichola Ashby

Nils Junge

Nina Shandloff

Oliver Goodworth

Pam Jones

Patricia McAuley

Paul Burlacu

Penny Tompkins & James Lawley

Peter Ng

Phoebe Macdonald

Rebecca Hoang

Regula Carratu

Renelle Tarnowska

Rhian Pritchard

Robert McNally

Ruth Murray

Sara Goodworth

Sarah Eze

Sarah Free

Sarah Young,

Saskia Zoet

Sharon Baker

Sharon Small

Sheila Ford

Shona Yee

Simon Bor

Simon Maydon

Steve Craig

Stuart Sew Hoy

Sue Corkill

Sue Roper

Sukyee Law

Susie Kong

Teresa Barnard

Theresa Booth

Thulasi Mohanadas

Tiggy Munnelly

Tim Berry	Veronica Dunn
Timothy Shue	Wallace Sew Hoy
Tyrone Sew Hoy	Wendy Reardon
Val Lurcook	Yujin Kim

My gratitude also to friends, colleagues, and classmates in my various communities of support who have endured listening to me waxing lyrically about my writing and publishing journey: my fellow Toastmaster members at The Reigate Rhetoric and Epsom Speakers Clubs, Vege Book Club, Coaches Book Club, Clean Campus community, Lockdown Ladies, St. George's Hill Golf Club, and the Field of Fitness.

All of you have played a part in helping me give birth to this book. It's been a long gestation period, and I'm looking forward to seeing how this baby grows and develops!

Thank you for reading my book.

If you have any comments, feedback, or questions, do contact me.

I'd love to know your thoughts and feelings about what you've read and what difference this is making for you.

Contact me at: doris@dorissewhoy.com

Or connect with me on social media:

LinkedIn: Doris Sew Hoy

Facebook: /doris.sewhoy

Instagram: @dorissewhoy

APPENDIX

INTRODUCTION

Cambridge Dictionary. s.v. "awareness (*n.*)." Accessed January 26, 2022. https://dictionary.cambridge.org/us/dictionary/english/awareness.

Csikszentmihalyi, Mihaly. *Flow: The Psychology of Happiness.* London: Penguin Random House, 2002.

Grant, Adam. *Think Again: The Power of Knowing What You Don't Know.* London: Penguin Random House, 2021.

Randstat. "The Great Resignation: 69 Percent of UK Workers Ready to Move Job." Industry Insight. Last modified November 5, 2021. https://www.randstad.co.uk/about-us/industry-insight/great-resignation/.

Tzu, Lao. *The Way and Its Power: Lao Tzu's Tao Te Ching and Its Place in Chinese Thought.* Translated by Arthur Waley. Eastford: Martino Fine Books, 2016.

Wambach, Abby. *Wolfpack: How to Come Together, Unleash Our Power and Change the Game.* London: Little, Brown Book Group. 2019.

CHAPTER 1

Collins, Jim. *Beyond Entrepreneurship 2.0.* London: Penguin Random House. 2020.

Brown, Brené. *Rising Strong: How the Ability to Reset Transforms the Way We Live, Love, Parent, and Lead.* New York: Random House, 2017.

Lexico.com. s.v. "trust (n.)." Oxford: Oxford University Press, Accessed January 3, 2022. https://www.lexico.com/en/definition/trust.

O'Neill, Onora. "What We Don't Understand about Trust." Filmed June 2013 at TEDxHousesOfParliament, London, UK. Video, 09:38. https://www.ted.com/talks/onora_o_neill_what_we_don_t_understand_about_trust?source=email.

Sakulku, Jaruwan and James Alexander. "The Impostor Phenomenon." *International Journal of Behavioral Science* 6, no. 1 (2011), 75-97. https://doi.org/10.14456/ijbs.2011.6.

CHAPTER 2

Gianasso, Guido. "Emma Raducanu and the Illusion of Nations. A New Tennis Champion Has Emerged. It Is Fascinating to Observe the Dynamics Taking Place around This Young Lady." LinkedIn, September 2021. https://www.linkedin.com/posts/guidogianasso_emma-raducanu-and-the-illusion-of-nations-activity-6844951439719190528-kpi5/.

Myers, Isabel Briggs and Peter B. Myers. *Gifts Differing: Understanding Personality Type.* Palo Alto: Davies-Black Publishing, 1980.

Tolle, Eckhart. *The Power of Now: A Guide to Spiritual Enlightenment.* San Francisco: New World Library, 1999.

CHAPTER 3

Brainy Quote. "Virgil Thompson." Accessed January 5, 2022. https://www.brainyquote.com/quotes/virgil_thomson_163833.

Brown, Brené. *Dare to Lead: Brave Work. Tough Conversations. Whole Hearts.* London: Penguin Random House, 2018.

Eastwood, Owen. *Belonging: The Ancient Code of Togetherness.* London: Quercus, 2021.

Luft, Joe and Harry Ingham. "The Johari Window: A Graphic Model of Awareness in Group Relations." *Proceedings of the Western Training Laboratory in Group Development.* Los Angeles: UCLA, 1955.

Poole, Eve. *Leadersmithing: Revealing the Trade Secrets of Leadership.* London: Bloomsbury Business, 2017.

Roberts, Mere. "Ways of Seeing: Whakapapa." *A Journal of Social Anthropology and Cultural Studies* 10, no. 1 (January 2013): 93-120. https://www.researchgate.net/publication/270771663_Ways_of_Seeing_Whakapapa.

Sew Hoy-Agnew, Jenny and Trevor Agnew. *Merchant, Miner, Mandarin: The Life and Times of the Remarkable Choie Sew Hoy.* Christchurch: University of Canterbury Press, 2020.

Stephens, Georgia. "I'm from Iran You Say?" *The Sunday Times*; September 26, 2021. https://www.thetimes.co.uk/article/exploring-my-heritage-on-a-london-based-tour-of-iran-h33t29fx5.

CHAPTER 4

Frankl, Viktor E. *Man's Search for Meaning.* Boston: Beacon Press, 2006.

Karpman, Stephen B. "Fairy Tales and Script Drama Analysis." *Transactional Analysis Bulletin* 7, no. 26 (1968): 39-43.

Low, Phillip. "Overview of the Autonomic Nervous System." Merck Manual Professional Version. Kenilworth: Merck & Co., Inc, 2020.

Maclean, Paul. "The Truine Brain." *The Science of Psychotherapy* (blog). October 26, 2016. Accessed January 19, 2022. https://www.thescienceofpsychotherapy.com/the-triune-brain/.

Porges, Stephen W. *The Pocket Guide to The Polyvagal Theory: The Transformative Power of Feeling Safe.* New York: W. W. Norton & Company Ltd, 2017.

Sapolskey, Robert. *Behave.* Penguin Press, 2017.

Vaughan Smith, Julia. *Coaching and Trauma: From Surviving to Thriving.* Maidenhead: Open University Press, 2019.

CHAPTER 5

Linley, Alex, Janet Willars, and Robert Biswas-Diener. *The Strengths Book: Be Confident, Be Successful, and Enjoy Better Relationships by Realizing the Best of You.* CAPP Press, 2010.

Peterson, Christopher and Martin Seligman. *Character Strengths and Virtues: A Handbook and Classification.* Washington DC: American Psychological Association, 2004.

Williamson, Marianne. *A Return to Love: Reflections on the Principles of "A Course in Miracles."* New York: Harper One, 1996.

CHAPTER 6

Geary, James. *I Is an Other: The Secret Life of Metaphor and How It Shapes the Way We See the World.* New York: Harper Perennial, 2011.

Goldsmith, Dafanie. "Obituary of David Grove." The Clean Collection. Accessed January 12, 2022. https://cleanlanguage.co.uk/articles/articles/283/1/Obituary-of-David-Grove-1950-2008/Page1.html.

Lakoff, George and Mark Johnson. *Metaphors We Live By.* Chicago: The University of Chicago Press, 1980.

Lawley, James and Penny Tompkins. *Metaphors in the Mind: Transformation Through Symbolic Modelling.* London: The Developing Company Press, 2000.

Walker, Caitlin. *From Curiosity to Contempt: Creating the Conditions for Groups to Collaborate.* Hampshire: Clean Publishing, 2014.

Whitmore, John. *Coaching for Performance: GROWing Human Potential and Purpose—The Principles and Practice of Coaching and Leadership, 4th Edition.* London: Nicholas Brealey Publishing, 2009.

Wilson, Carol. *The Work and Life of David Grove: Clean Language and Emergent Knowledge.* Kibworth: Troubador Publishing Ltd, 2017.

CHAPTER 7

Aydemir, Omer and Ilkin Icelli. "Burnout: Risk Factors." *Burnout for Experts: Prevention in the Context of Living and Working* 1, no. 1 (2013): 119-143. https://link.springer.com/chapter/10.1007%2F978-1-4614-4391-9_8.

Eagleman, David M., Peter U. Tse, Dean Buonomano, Peter Janssen, Anna Christina Nobre and Alex O. Holcombe. "Time and the Brain: How Subjective Time Relates to Neural Time." *Journal of Neuroscience* 25, no. 45 (November 2005): 10369–10371. https://www.jneurosci.org/content/25/45/10369.

Encyclopedia.com. s.v. "construct (n.)." Accessed January 13, 2022. https://www.encyclopedia.com/science-and-technology/computers-and-electrical-engineering/computers-and-computing/construct.

Freudenberger, Herbert J. "Staff Burnout." *Journal of Social Issues* 30, no. 1 (1974): 159-165. https://doi.org/10.1111/j.1540-4560.1974.tb00706.x.

Lexico. s.v. "serentity (n.)" Oxford: Oxford University Press, Accessed January 13, 2022. https://www.lexico.com/en/definition/serenity.

Pálsdóttir, Anna María, Dennis Persson, Birgitta Persson, and Patrik Grahn. "The Journey of Recovery and Empowerment Embraced by Nature—Clients' Perspectives on Nature-Based Rehabilitation in Relation to the Role of the Natural Environment." *International Journal of Environmental Research and Public Health* 11, no. 7 (July 2014): 7094-7115. https://doi.org/10.3390/ijerph110707094.

Searles, Harold. "Unconscious Processes in Relation to the Environmental Crisis." *Psychoanalytic Review* 59, no. 3 (1972): 361–374. https://pep-web.org/browse/document/psar.059.0361a?page=P0361.

Shapiro, Fred R. "Who Wrote the Serenity Prayer?" *The Chronicle of Higher Education*, April 28, 2014. https://www.chronicle.com/article/who-wrote-the-serenity-prayer/.

Sifton, Elisabeth. *The Serenity Prayer: Faith and Politics in Times of Peace and War.* New York: W. W. Norton & Company, 2005.

Stuart-Smith, Sue. *The Well Gardened Mind: Rediscovering Nature in the Modern World.* Glasgow: William Collins, 2020.

CHAPTER 8

Baume, David. "A Dynamic Theory of Organizational Knowledge Creation." *Organization Science* 5, no. 1 (February 1994): 14-37.

Broadwell, Martin M. "Teaching for Learning (XVI)." *The Gospel Guardian* 20, no. 41 (February 20, 1969): 1-3a.

Edmondson, Amy C. *The Fearless Organization: Creating Psychological Safety in the Workplace for Learning, Innovation, and Growth.* Hoboken: John Wiley & Sons, 2018.

Hudson, Therese. *Let's Talk: Make Effective Feedback Your Superpower.* New York: Penguin Random House, 2021.

McLeod, Saul. "Humanistic Approach." Simply Psychology. Last modified 2020. https://www.simplypsychology.org/humanistic.html.

Online Etymology Dictionary. s.v. "compassion (*n.*)." Accessed January 24, 2022. https://www.etymonline.com/word/compassion.

Online Etymology Dictionary. s.v. "empathy (*n.*)." Accessed January 24, 2022. https://www.etymonline.com/word/empathy.

Remen, Rachel Naomi. *Kitchen Table Wisdom: Stories That Heal, 10th Anniversary Edition.* New York: Penguin Random House, 2006.

CHAPTER 9

Brackett, Marc. *Permission to Feel: Unlock the Power of Emotions to Help Yourself and Your Child Thrive.* New York: Celadon Books, 2019.

Colman, Andrew. *A Dictionary of Psychology 3rd Ed.* Oxford: Oxford University Press, 2008.

Goleman, Daniel. *Emotional Intelligence: Why It Can Matter More Than IQ.* New York: Bantam Books, 1995.

Rosenburg, Marshall B. *Nonviolent Communication: A Language of Life, Third Edition.* Encinitas: PuddleDancer Press, 2015.

Zhao, Chloé. "Oscars 2021: Chloé Zhao, from Outsider to Hollywood History-Maker." *BBC News*, April 26, 2021. https://www.bbc.co.uk/news/entertainment-arts-56828748.amp.

CHAPTER 10

Christensen, Lisa, Jake Gittleson and Matt Smith. "The Most Fundamental Skill: Intentional Learning and the Career Advantage." *McKinsey Quarterly,* August 7, 2020. https://www.mckinsey.com/featured-insights/future-of-work/the-most-fundamental-skill-intentional-learning-and-the-career-advantage.

Dunbar, R.I. *How Many Friends Does One Person Need? Dunbar's Number and Other Evolutionary Quirks.* London: Faber and Faber, 2011.

Dweck, Carol. *Mindset: The New Psychology of Success.* New York: Random House, 2006.

Grant, Karina. "Interview with Simon Woodroffe— Founder of YO! Sushi." *HI CHI Life* (blog). 2021. https://hichi-life.com/blog/interview-with-simon-woodroffe-founder-of-yo-sushi/.

Lexico. s.v. "resilience (*n.*)." Oxford: Oxford University Press, Accessed January 13, 2022. https://www.lexico.com/en/definition/resilience.

Machin, Anna. *Why We Love: The New Science Behind Our Closest Relationships.* New York: Pegasus Books, 2022.

Malone-Kircher, Madison. "James Dyson on 5,126 Vacuums That Didn't Work— And the One the Finally Did." *New York Magazine,* November 22, 2016. https://nymag.com/vindicated/2016/11/james-dyson-on-5-126-vacuums-that-didnt-work-and-1-that-did.html.

Poole, Eve. *Leadersmithing: Revealing the Trade Secrets of Leadership.* London: Bloomsbury Business, 2017.

Stibel, Jeff. "Michael Jordan: A Profile in Failure." *CSQ Magazine,* August 29, 2017. https://csq.com/2017/08/michael-jordan-profile-failure/#.Yg_Gnt_P2Ul.

CHAPTER 11

Garcia, Hector and Francesc Miralles. *IKIGAI: The Japanese Secret to a Long and Happy Life.* London: Penguin Random House, 2016.

Goleman, Daniel and Richard J. Davidson. *The Science of Meditation: How to Change Your Brain, Mind, and Body.* London: Penguin Random House, 2017.

Suni, Eric. "How Much Sleep Do We Really Need?" *Sleep Foundation.* Updated March 10, 2021. https://www.sleepfoundation.org/how-sleep-works/how-much-sleep-do-we-really-need.

Thich Nhat Hanh. *The Way Out Is In: The Zen Calligraphy of the Father of Mindfulness.* London: Thames and Hudson Ltd. 2015.

William Yensen. "Opening to the Unknown—Body-Oriented Meditation." March 27, 2021. Video, 21:24. https://www.youtube.com/watch?v=luWH_zZ9Vww&ab_channel=WilliamYensen.

EPILOGUE

Harland, Philip. *Trust Me, I'm the Patient: Clean Language, Metaphor, and the New Psychology of Change.* London: Wayfinder Press, 2012.

Printed in Great Britain
by Amazon